Can
We
Do
That?

ndy Stanley

Ed Young

Can We Do That?

24

innovative practices that will change
the way you do church

Our purpose at Howard Publishing is to:

• *Increase faith* in the hearts of growing Christians
• *Inspire holiness* in the lives of believers
• *Instill hope* in the hearts of struggling people everywhere
  Because He's coming again!

Can We Do That? © 2002 by Edwin B. Young and C. Andrew Stanley
All rights reserved. Printed in the United States of America

Published by Howard Publishing Co., Inc.
3117 North 7th Street, West Monroe, Louisiana 71291-2227

03 04 05 06 07 08 09 10 11   10 9 8 7 6 5 4 3

Edited by Michele Buckingham
Interior design by Stephanie Denney

ISBN: 1-58229-238-8

contents

section 1 reaching out

section 4 getting the message across

acknowledgments

It is impossible to write a book like this without depending on the gifts, talents, insights, and dedication of many people over many years of ministry. Each one of these practices comes out of a real ministry run by real, dedicated staff and laypeople. We owe a debt of gratitude to all of the people, too numerous to name, from Fellowship Church and North Point Community Church who have contributed ideas over the years that are now published in this book.

We also want to acknowledge the many hours of hard work by assistants and editors, Diane Grant (NPCC), Jessica Lonsdale, and Cliff McNeely (FC), who have helped us harness and organize these ideas into black and white.

And I (Ed) would like to thank Andy personally for coming up with the idea to put these ideas in writing so that we could share them with others.

introduction

Andy Stanley

In the spring of 2000, Sandra and I had the privilege of vacationing for five days with Ed Young and his wife, Lisa. Thanks to the generosity of a family in our church, the four of us were able to relish the beauty and cuisine of the Cayman Islands.

However, what was intended to be a relaxing, non-ministry respite turned out to be one of the most challenging and stimulating series of conversations I have ever had in my life. Listening to Ed was like drinking from a fire hydrant. Over and over I heard myself saying, "That's a great idea, Ed. We ought to do that at North Point." And every once in a while, just to humor me, he would acknowledge one of my ideas as being helpful as well. What a guy. Anyway, by the end of the week, we both had a dozen or so "great" ideas to take back home and put into practice both personally and professionally.

On the last night of our mini-conference, it occurred to me, why not share these ideas with the rest of the world? After all, if we found these ideas to be fresh and relevant, perhaps other church leaders would as well. That's how this book was born.

There is no such thing as a one-size-fits-all ministry. You are intuitive enough to know which of our ideas will and will not work in your ministry environments. In fact, throughout the book, Ed and I have indicated how we might do things differently at our respective churches for each particular practice. We recognize that there is more than one way to do church. What works at North Point may not work at Fellowship, and vice versa. We assume that you will adapt these ideas to fit your personality and ministry style. For example, Ed attempted to ride a camel named Harpo into their worship center on a Sunday morning to illustrate his message. Someone as sophisticated as I am would never stoop to such a level. But then again, Ed has over 15,000 people showing up for his weekend services.

So we hope you find at least some of this information helpful. Use what you can. Improve on it. Most importantly, we hope it will motivate you to always strive for a better way to do this incredible God-given thing called church.

Dual authorship can be tricky. To keep things simple Ed and I will identify ourselves by our respective churches. When you see "at Fellowship Church" or "FC," you are hearing from Ed. When you see "at North Point Community Church" or "NPCC," that's me. Much of the text of this book was received in interview format. For that reason the writing style will vary. But who cares?

section 1

reaching out

invest and invite

Andy Stanley

We partner with our regular attenders to reach the unchurched.

At North Point Community Church, our evangelism strategy is summed up in two words: invest and invite. From the very beginning, we've told our people that our desire is to partner with them in the process of evangelism. As I am fond of saying, "We will do what you are afraid or unequipped to do: raise the issues. You do what we cannot do: invite your friends." As a result of this partnership, we see a high percentage of our people participating in personal evangelism. More than 90 percent of the adults we baptize came to NPCC at the invitation of a friend.

Fear and Ignorance

Let's face it, fear and ignorance are the two primary obstacles to personal evangelism. When I was growing up, leaders addressed these problems through training and motivation. In the 1970s and '80s, several excellent evangelism-training programs were developed to help believers overcome their fear and ignorance. Pastors preached compelling messages about reaching the lost and the need for all of us to personally embrace the Great Commission.

For some—primarily those with the gift of evangelism—it took. But most of us simply had to face the fact that we were cowards. We just could not bring ourselves to whip out a tract and present the gospel to our neighbors and friends. We accepted the fact that our Christian experience would include a measure of guilt regarding our lack of concern for the lost.

Investing in Lives

North Point's invest-and-invite strategy has made it safe for hundreds of seasoned but scared believers to get back into the game. Instead of training our people in the art of personal evangelism, we instruct them to invest in the lives of unbelievers with the express purpose of inviting them to an event where they will be exposed to the gospel in a clear, creative, and compelling manner. Is there a need for training? Yes. But our strategy is not dependent upon training. It is dependent upon purposeful relationships.

Believers are responsible for leveraging their relational influence for the sake of the kingdom of God. That's the part they can do that we—the church—can't. I have gone so far as to tell our folks that if they are not willing to leverage their influence for the kingdom, they are attending the wrong church. I don't want to raise money and build buildings so we can seat more note takers. Our mission is to lead people into a growing relationship with Christ. We operate off the premise that all regular attenders have embraced that mission as their own.

They are not responsible for knowing the answers to every question their unbelieving friends may throw their way. But they are responsible for exposing them to an environment where they will be presented with the gospel. Anybody can do that, assuming there is a church close by that is designed with the unchurched in mind.

Extending an Invitation

What we have discovered (and we certainly aren't the first) is that far more personal evangelism takes place if believers feel the freedom to invite their unbelieving friends to church. It is easier to invite people to an event than it is to confront them about their personal belief system. It is easier to include them in on something you are excited about than it is to convince them that their entire world-view is incorrect.

While we do not do "seeker services," we do design our weekend services with the "investee" in mind. We assume that every Sunday morning hundreds of our people are going to show up with that friend, neighbor, or family member with whom they have been cultivating a relationship. Often people will introduce me to their guest and, without saying it directly,

3

let me know that this is their investee. What they are really saying is, "I finally got 'em here. Don't blow it for me!"

The Eye of the Beholder

Our goal for our unchurched guests is to create a comfortable environment where they are confronted with the intensely practical nature of the Scripture. I want them to leave thinking, *I didn't know that was in there. That was actually helpful.*

Evangelism is a process. Establishing the relevance of the Bible is often a necessary precursor to convincing people of its divine source. Our church is inundated with people who have not yet put their faith in Christ for salvation but whose lives are slowly being transformed by the application of God's Word.

Exposing unbelievers to the relevance of Scripture is something the church can do a better job of than the individual believer. This is why partnership evangelism is so effective.

Back to You

At the end of our worship services, we place the responsibility of evangelism squarely on the shoulders of our people. I do this as conspicuously as possible. I say things like, "If you have any questions about what you have heard this morning, ask the person who invited you. They will do a far better job explaining it than I did" or "The person who invited you this morning would love to discuss this with you over lunch."

On several occasions members have come up to me before a service and asked me to make one of those statements. They were looking for an opportunity—an opening—to take the conversation with their investee to a new level. They understood what it meant to partner with the church in evangelism.

Less Is More

One other advantage of our invest-and-invite strategy is that it is an easy plan to communicate. It is not seven steps or five steps; it is two words. Everybody in our church knows what I am talking about when I refer to our invest-and-invite strategy. And everybody knows whether or not they are on board with us.

In our elders' meetings, we keep up with and pray for each other's investees. The same is true in our staff meetings. Leaders (including staff) know that on the Sunday their investee shows up, they are released from their normal ministry duties. Their responsibility on that Sunday is to navigate their friend through a morning at NPCC and then go have lunch.

Every church needs an evangelism strategy that the members understand and embrace. Our invest-and-invite strategy is easy to communicate and easy to apply. More importantly, it reflects one of the first instances of evangelism in the New Testament. When Andrew discovered Jesus' true identity, the Bible says he went and found his brother Peter, and "he brought him to Jesus" (John 1:42).

The church is the body of Christ. Bringing the unchurched in among the body is the next best thing to bringing them to the person of Jesus.

ED'S TAKE

Like Andy, I believe the role of evangelism is a nonnegotiable in the local church. Every church should have as part of its purpose a statement about evangelism. One of our stated purposes at Fellowship Church is "to reach out and share the good news of Jesus Christ." Unfortunately, churches often fall victim to the navel-gazing principle; when left on their own, they turn inward and become a holy huddle with an "us four and no more" mentality.

One of the primary responsibilities of the senior pastor and staff is to keep the church focused on evangelism. Many churches teach the importance of reaching out but fail miserably in modeling evangelism to the church. I recognize that it is difficult for church staff to witness and invite people to come to church because we spend most of our time around church people. When I started Fellowship, I decided early on that I would spend a good deal of my time around people who were not Christians. Wherever I go—the health club, restaurants, the theater, sporting events, etc.—I constantly invite people I meet to attend Fellowship Church. I tell them about how Christ can change their lives.

We hold our staff accountable for the contacts they have

with unchurched people. Often in staff meetings, I will go around the room and ask staff members to report on who they are spending time with. If staff members are not talking to people who are hell bound, then something's out of balance in their schedule and priorities.

A Tag-Team Event

Not only do I encourage our staff to share the good news of Christ, I regularly challenge the congregation to invite their friends, family, and coworkers to Fellowship. I promise our regular attendees that if they will invite someone to Fellowship, we will make sure that the moment their friend or family member pulls into the parking lot, he or she will feel comfortable and welcome. More importantly, we will make sure that all visitors hear that God created them, Christ died for them, and He is the only way to eternity in heaven.

I tell our congregation that evangelism is a tag-team event. It takes both the staff and the congregation to work together to get people to visit our church.

A healthy church should have a mixture of three groups of people attending: those who have not stepped over the line of faith, those who have just made a faith reception, and those who are mature in their faith. If everyone is a mature believer, you are not doing the Great Commission. Conversely, if the church is full of baby believers, you are not discipling.

I've also discovered that the best way to market the church is through word-of-mouth advertising. Our surveys indicate that 98 percent of the people who attend FC showed up for the first time because someone invited them. If you have a church that is creative, relevant, and exciting to attend, people will invite their friends—that's a given. If your church is boring and irrelevant, you can have evangelism classes 24/7 and it won't matter. People will not invite others to a boring church.

2

targeting the unchurched

Ed Young

*We focus on making the unchurched visitor
feel welcome and comfortable.*

At Fellowship Church our vision is to reach up, reach out, and reach in. By "reaching up," we mean worshiping God. By "reaching out," we are talking about evangelism. And by "reaching in," we are referring to discipleship.

That second factor, "reaching out," is critical. We are an evangelism-driven church, and we truly believe that we should be reaching and saving the unchurched in our community. Our perspective at Fellowship is that there is simply no excuse for our church not to grow.

Let me ask a direct question. Why are you in the ministry? Why do you feel called to be a leader of the church? Is it so that you can wallow around in a massive bog of paperwork? Because you enjoy the 3 A.M. phone calls with someone sobbing hysterically on the other end of the line? To ensure that people will look at you aghast when you answer the cheery question, "So what do you do for a living?"

The reason I am in the ministry is because there is nothing, absolutely nothing on earth, like seeing someone come to Christ. I work hard because I am working for people's salvation. Prayerfully, that is your ultimate motivation too. Why be in the ministry if you are not going to give more than your all to influence eternity? My church, your church, must be designed to reach out to people in the community.

Be Creative

For that reason, everything we do at Fellowship Church is tailored to communicate to someone who has never darkened a church door in his or her life. Our signs, direct mail, bulletins, messages, worship service, the words we use, the timing of our teaching series, programming—all are geared toward the seeker. Consider:

- Signs that are large, clear, and colorful

- Direct-mail flyers that are vibrant, compelling, informative, and easy to understand

- Bulletins that are eye catching and play up the excitement of what the church has to offer

- A message on a relevant topic (such as sex or honesty) that doesn't focus on, or even use, complicated theological terms

- Bible verses flashed up on the side screens for those who don't have a Bible

- Culturally relevant music—for example, having the music team sing Pink Floyd's "Brick in the Wall" before a message on discipline

- A series on parenting that starts on Mother's Day, when plenty of unchurched families will have been dragged to church by moms who "just want to have a nice Sunday for once!"

- Three Newcomers Classes a month (one Saturday night, one Sunday afternoon, one Tuesday night) to accommodate everyone's schedules

These are the kinds of things we do at Fellowship Church, and almost all are explored in further detail in other chapters. But the overall strategy is clear: Keep evangelism at the forefront.

Be Intentional

Put yourself in a visitor's place. Visit another church in the area and see how it feels, noting how you would do things differently. If people don't feel a part of something, they're not very likely to come back to it.

That's the reason we no longer have a denominational tie-in in our church name. For the first year or so of our life, we were

Las Colinas Baptist Church. Gradually, the "Baptist" got smaller and smaller, until finally we decided to drop it.

Fellowship Church is part of the Southern Baptist Convention, which allows a lot of individual church autonomy. But unfortunately, people have a lot of preconceptions about denominations. And whether or not those preconceptions are correct, they are a stumbling block and a barrier to many people. If someone were to look at the name Las Colinas Baptist Church and think, *Baptists are too stuffy* (this is not my opinion, but it may be what a seeker believes), we would lose that person. I'm not saying all churches should drop the denominational references in their names, but we must be very sensitive to how the denominational tie-in is perceived by the unchurched and work to overcome any misconceptions that might exist.

Be a Model

Ultimately, senior pastors must be a model of evangelism. They must be willing to be put in situations with people in the community and be comfortable saying, "Hey, I'm a pastor. Come visit the church sometime." In fact, senior pastors should spend more time with the lost and unchurched than they do with church members. They must be people who have the gift of leadership, who love to be around people, and who love to talk and communicate God's life-giving message.

This will play out in different ways for different personalities. One of the best things Fellowship Church did along these lines was to give me a membership to the local sports club. I love to work out, and I've been able to meet plenty of people who would never have heard of our church otherwise. For some pastors, opportunities may come through playing golf with different people in the community. For others, it may come through those casual conversations with the dry cleaner, the grocery clerk, the auto mechanic, or anyone else they come in contact with on a regular basis.

A few years back, I was sitting in a carpool line at my daughter's elementary school, waiting to pick her up, when I saw someone that caught my attention. A man was waiting by his car for his children, and I could tell by his appearance, by the way he handled himself, that he did not know Christ personally. I'd never seen him before, but I felt like God was telling me to pray for him. So without having any direct contact with this man, I began to pray for him regularly. For one year I wrote in my journal, "God, give me an opportunity to talk to this man about you."

Then one Sunday morning as I was teaching, I scanned the crowd and saw the man I'd been praying for sitting in the fourth row. A month later we had lunch, and over the meal he committed his life to Jesus Christ. In a letter I recently received from his wife, I found out that my prayers were only part of God's plan for this man. Unbeknownst to me, his family had been attending Fellowship Church for several months. And because of the change he'd seen in them, he began to attend the church himself. I was privileged to ultimately lead him to a saving knowledge of Christ.

Restoring Vitality to Ministry

Our communities are full of people who, like this father sitting in a carpool line, need to hear that Jesus loves them and has a wonderful plan for their lives. If we as pastors and churches aren't sensitive to reaching out to, praying for, and welcoming in the lost, then we are missing something vital in our ministry.

Whether or not your church is labeled as "seeker sensitive" is not the issue. The important thing is that your ministry is designed with the unchurched person in mind. We target the unchurched at Fellowship because that's what Christ did. Christ came to seek and to save those who are lost; and as representatives of Christ on the earth, we must extend that same hand to a lost and dying world.

ANDY'S TAKE

I often encourage pastors to invite unchurched neighbors to come and evaluate their services—to come as secret shoppers. Most of us have been believers for so long that we really cannot identify with emotional and intellectual obstacles that keep the unchurched away. Evaluating our churches through the eyes and ears of the unchurched is both necessary and painful!

videotaped baptism testimonies

Andy Stanley

We videotape baptism testimonies and use them as an evangelistic tool during baptismal services.

At North Point Community Church, we require baptism candidates to allow us to videotape their testimonies. Each testimony is then played in the Sunday morning worship service immediately preceding the person's actual baptism.

These videos vary in length from thirty seconds to four minutes. Sometimes they are as simple as: "Hello, my name is Jeff Smith. I am here to declare my love for Jesus Christ by publicly identifying with him through baptism. Thank you for sharing this important moment with me." Other times, candidates share the entire story of how they came to Christ.

Take Fifteen

Candidates are allowed to record and re-record their stories as many times as they like. One lady did fifteen takes. She was so emotional that she would actually get up and leave the room in the middle of her story. That was OK with us. The emotion and sincerity behind the words are what make this practice so impacting. Finally, on the fifteenth take, she was able to hold back her tears long enough to get through to the end.

She invited her father and mother to attend her baptism. Her father refused to come, but her seventy-three-year-old unchurched mom came. She has been coming ever since. Three weeks later her father reluctantly agreed to attend North Point, and he, too, continued to show up on a regular basis. Nine months later I had the privilege of leading this eighty-two-year-old man in the sinner's prayer. Yeah, God!

Eternal Impact

We record baptism videos immediately following our two Sunday morning worship services—usually four to eight people per session. Before we begin recording, we show the candidates an eight-minute bloopers video. This hilarious presentation includes both instruction and examples of how not to do a baptism video.

We encourage candidates to include two things in their address. First, we feel it is important for them to mention the fact that they have entered into a personal relationship with Jesus Christ. Second, we encourage them to thank the people who were instrumental in leading them to Christ or to our church. Nothing inspires our people to embrace relational evangelism like these stories. Week after week they are exposed to real people whose lives have been eternally impacted by a simple invitation to visit a church service.

We usually record the videos two weeks prior to the actual baptism ceremony, giving us time to determine the order in which the testimonies should be played. As you might guess, we try to save the best for last. A compelling adult conversion testimony opens the hearts of unbelievers to the possibility that there just may be something to all of this. Consequently, I make my strongest evangelistic appeals immediately following baptism.

Say Cheese

Not everybody is excited about being on the big screen. Occasionally someone will ask if they can skip the video portion and just be baptized. To date, we have made no exceptions to our video requirement. When people express concern about doing the video, we invite them to attend a taping session so they can see what goes on behind the scenes. Once they see the relaxed, friendly atmosphere in which we tape, they always agree to "give it a try." We have never had an adult refuse baptism because of the video.

The other thing we do to encourage people to follow through with the video is to remind them of the potential impact their stories could have. To drive the point home even further, we always remind candidates, "You may never again have an opportunity to share the difference Christ has made in your life with several thousand people. And you never know who may step across the line of faith because of something you say." That's not hype. That's the truth. And since most of these people have attended worship services where we have baptized people, they know the potential impact of their testimonies.

Children's Baptism

We handle children's baptism a little differently. In fact, we rarely baptize children during a Sunday morning service. Instead, once a quarter we put together a giant Birthday Party. This is a Sunday afternoon event where we dedicate babies and baptize children. In effect, we celebrate physical and spiritual births. After the service, we send parents and children out by age groups to designated parts of the building where they eat birthday cake and ice cream.

Children are required to do a video as well. These are generally much shorter and much cuter than the adult versions. Each child is given a copy of his or her video to keep. My two sons have watched their videos about a hundred times apiece. As you might imagine, having a videotape of our children's testimonies is something my wife, Sandra, and I will treasure forever. And when they hit adolescence, we may require them to watch it every night before bedtime.

Weekend Highlight

At NPCC we baptize every other Sunday morning. We usually baptize anywhere from four to seven people per service. On those weekends, we include an information piece in our bulletin explaining the ordinance of baptism. This explanation, along with the videos, generates 90 percent of our baptisms. Because we give candidates an opportunity to share their stories, baptism has become a highlight of our weekend services.

ED'S TAKE

Baptismal services are definitely a time of celebration at Fellowship Church. We baptized almost sixteen hundred people in the last year, so as you might imagine, we tend to hold baptisms rather frequently. Generally, we have a baptism service after our First Wednesday service (a time of concentrated worship the first Wednesday night of every month), and another after the Saturday night and Sunday morning services later in the month. A typical service may baptize anywhere from forty to fifty people and can even go up to several hundred.

In the beginning we used swimming pools and hot tubs to baptize. When we built our facility, however, we decided to place an outdoor fountain near the worship center that could be used for baptisms year-round. When not in use, metal grates are placed in the fountain to keep people—children especially—from trying to jump in the water. When in use, the grates are removed, and there is enough room to baptize two people at a time. The fountain is heated in the winter for maximum comfort.

Because the fountain is located outside the worship center, thousands of people walk by the baptism service on their way to the parking lot or to the preschool building. It's a very public way to promote the significance of baptism. Chances are, many of the spectators have no clue about what baptism by immersion is all about. When we have a baptismal celebration, I (or another pastor) talk to the spectators about what baptism means and explain its spiritual importance.

We also make a baptismal celebration the theme of at least two weekend services each year. These big events are immensely popular. Hundreds of people are baptized during these services, and thousands more watch the celebration.

I always preach a message on salvation and/or baptism first and then promote the next weekend as the special celebration. People are invited to fill out an insert in the bulletin or to register on-line to be baptized. Our staff also calls baptismal candidates to encourage them to be baptized during this event. All candidates give us a written account of their stories—when they became Christ-followers, how their lives have changed since their decision, and what Fellowship Church means to them.

For these big celebrations, we use portable tanks set up on the stage to do the baptisms. During the services we read testimonies of how and when people became Christ-followers. Sometimes we show video testimonies of the life changes people have experienced since becoming followers of Christ. We broadcast these baptismal services live or delayed on our Web site so that family members across the world can watch.

If baptism services become "big events," people will get excited about being a part of something special. There's no better way to reach people and promote the importance of baptism than by making it a significant event in the life of the church.

4

streaming video

Ed Young

*We stream baptisms, dedication services,
and sermons on the Internet.*

Fellowship Church's Web site, www.fellowshipchurch.com, gets over 125,000 hits a day. It has links to just about everything you can think of related to our church: our vision, our location, our staff, our different departments, the message of salvation, sermon notes and transcripts, tapes, and on and on. Furthermore, we use real-time streaming video technology to run videos of certain services and baptisms live on the Internet. Anyone with access to an Internet connection can link up to what we're doing right at that moment.

Reaching Friends and Family

As with everything we do, the Bible is the driving force behind our effort to stream our baptisms. Being baptized is a litmus test of the Christian faith, and we should keep it a high priority. It's a public profession of faith—and let's face it, making a baptism available to the entire Internet population is surely the ultimate in going public. It's a witness of enormous proportions.

People can casually mention to their friends that they are being baptized and would love them to see it—if not at the church, then from the comfort of their own homes. Once these friends have logged on to the Web site to watch the baptism, they may start checking out other aspects of the church. Over two thousand people viewed the huge indoor baptism ceremony we streamed not long ago, and we received plenty of e-mails thanking us for giving them that opportunity.

Family members appreciate this option as well. Extended families today are spread out all across the country. Relatives who want to see their loved ones being baptized can't always hop on their planes, trains, and automobiles and show up at our church. We also stream our child dedications live every Mother's Day for the same reason.

Church for Out-of-Towners

Recognizing that we live in a very transient, mobile society, we've put a link to our weekend message on-line. That way, a businesswoman who is out of town on Sunday morning can check the Web site at her leisure and watch the service any time that week. Or someone who was actually at the service but who wanted to review it—to hear a certain part of the message again or to clarify something that was confusing—could go back and listen to it on the Internet.

Again, this is a very nonthreatening way of reaching people. They have the ability to check out Fellowship Church in the comfort of their homes, any time they want to, just sitting at their computer—in their pajamas, maybe, if they don't feel like getting dressed. They are able to "attend" the worship service without stepping out of their comfort zones. It is very intimate: At any time, in any place, they can look into what Fellowship Church is all about.

Technology and Technicalities

Our technology pastor is in charge of getting all of this information on the Internet. During a typical service, we have video cameras in the worship center showing the service on side screens. That video is on-line by about 2:00 Sunday afternoon and stays up until the next week's message is put in its place. My sermon notes are available along with the video for that week. Then the message is archived and available for purchase along with others in the form of transcripts, tapes, CDs, and videos in some cases.

Since there are so many different Internet connection speeds, we offer the on-line message in three formats: audio only, a slower video format (for 56K modems), and a high-speed video format (for DSL cable connections and faster).

Live, real-time streaming is a little more complex. If we are streaming something from the worship center—say, an indoor baptism or a baby dedication—then we use the side-screen video, encode it into a real-media format, and send it to the server. There's only a twenty-second delay. Because our video equipment is all indoors, we don't have the technology right now to make it feasible to stream outdoor baptisms or events— but we're getting there.

ANDY'S TAKE

North Point's Web site is designed primarily as a tool for our membership. We do on-line registration for all of our camps, shows, seasonal events, and even our monthly Area Fellowship meetings. Members and regular attenders can set up a "My NPCC" page that gives them the specific information they need without having to wade through the entire Web site.

Several times a year, we design a Web page that serves as an advertisement for an upcoming series. We e-mail our member- ship and regular attenders with a link to that site, and we encourage them to forward it to a friend along with a brief invi- tation to attend the series. This has been extraordinarily suc- cessful. Our folks say it has given them an easy and nonthreatening way to invite people to church. This creative use of technology in itself has sparked the interest of many unchurched people.

5

intentional marketing

Ed Young

We are intense about advertising our church to the community.

Marketing is something the secular world is very good at. The best companies are those that saturate the market with their name; when you walk down the toothpaste aisle, for example, you immediately recognize Crest and feel comfortable buying it. As people in our community walk down the aisle of life, what will pop into their heads when they feel like checking out a church? If we at Fellowship Church are marketing ourselves as we should, then they will think of us and feel comfortable visiting the church because they recognize the name.

From Billboards to Dot Coms

We advertise Fellowship Church through many different venues. We have shown slides before movies at nearby movie theaters. We have made flashy billboards that say "Fellowship reaching out

Church: Inner-tainment for the Heart." We have an ad in the Yellow Pages. We advertise in the high school football programs of nearby school districts. We make T-shirts for almost every activity we do—from our Beach Retreat to Vacation Bible School to basketball league games—so that when members wear the shirts, people see the name.

It's not that any of these ways of getting our name out is vital in itself; the idea is that all of them work together. Someone may see our billboard one day, then hear someone talking about us the next. Then they get a direct-mail flyer in their mailbox and think, *Huh. Maybe I should check these guys out.*

Churches should take every marketing avenue possible to reach their communities. One of the most interesting things we've done to market Fellowship Church is to paint our logo on top of the church building. We are situated less than five minutes from Dallas/Fort Worth International Airport, and several million people fly over us each year. So we hired a company that paints professional football end zones to paint "Fellowship Church" big enough for fliers to read as they cruise to a landing. What a fantastic way to reach people!

The city of Grapevine, where we are located, tried to keep us from painting the logo by citing some pretty obscure restrictions and rules, but our attorneys assured us we could go ahead. Several people have told us that seeing this logo was what enticed them to check out the church. This kind of creativity and drive is what gets the word out to people that something different happens within our walls.

Our most recent endeavor—I know you're going to think this is way out there (join the club!)—has been to change our logo to "fellowshipchurch.com." Starting in February 2001, we have been adding the logo to our building signs at the front and top of the worship center; on our letterhead, business cards, and brochures; and on everything else we print and distribute internally and externally to the public. We are not officially changing the name of the church, but we believe the net effect (pun intended) will be a consistent association between our Web address and our church name. The move received national and international attention (a reporter from South Africa even called us for an interview) before we officially launched our Web site.

People wonder if we ever are accused of being gimmicky. I say that it's great to be gimmicky. If you can communicate the truth of God's Word to your community through being gimmicky, if you can lead people to Jesus through being gimmicky, then go for it. I've learned not to be afraid of people hurling accusations at me, because that will happen no matter what I do. If you live in fear of criticism, you will never achieve God's vision for your life and church.

Of course, you have to strategically plan your exposure to fit your budget and resources. We used to hold a Fall Festival as an alternative to Halloween, but we don't anymore; it's a very expensive proposition and requires a lot of manpower. We don't want our church to become big-event driven. We want to communicate God's truth in a compelling way, and when big events help us with that, we'll use them. But we strategically choose what we want to focus on.

The Main Event

We have often used community-wide events to market ourselves. For example, at the time of the Persian Gulf War, our church was about eighteen months old and had seven or eight hundred people attending the services. With everyone's help we organized a "Celebrate Freedom" concert on the July 4th following the victory, and over 18,000 people showed up. It was an incredible experience. Right after the Oklahoma City bombing in 1995, we organized a basketball game to raise money for the victims: our church staff versus the Dallas Cowboys. (One of the Cowboys who attends our church helped our team out.) The press gave us great coverage, and we raised $25,000. Other events we've used include baseball clinics with professional baseball players, women's events like Creative Treasures (for making crafts during the holidays), and singles' weekends with music and seminars on dating and relationships.

Occasionally we tie a big event into a sermon series. When I did a series called Animal Planet, which focused on different animals in the Bible, we kicked it off with "Pet-a-palooza." We brought a petting zoo from the Fort Worth Zoo right into our lobby; we held animal contests; we had trainers and vets and plenty of food—for both animals and people. People came, brought their pets, and had a blast. Brute and Apollo, my two bull mastiffs that weigh 150 and 145 pounds respectively, were also present, and to my knowledge they only ate one kitten. (I'm kidding; that's a joke.)

What You Get

Big events reap incredible benefits. No matter the size of your congregation, you'll be amazed at what a community event will do to bring people into the church. We try to do big events right before a natural downfall in attendance, like spring break or the beginning of summer, and attendance always flourishes. Furthermore, people like to be part of something big, to work together for something that will truly advance the kingdom of God. A big event is a way for them to invite their friends to church for something nonthreatening. Plus, as we plan and organize these events, leaders rise to the surface. We discover wonderful laypeople we never would have before.

It's astonishing to me the lengths secular corporations will go to in order to market relatively insignificant products like deodorant or nail polish. The church has the most important, most compelling message ever—Jesus Christ—and we need to get that message out using every means possible so that lives can be changed.

ANDY'S TAKE

One of the differences between North Point Community Church and Fellowship Church is that Ed is constantly looking for new ways to capture new markets. He is very intentional about trying to expose unchurched people to the ministries of Fellowship Church. He has done a great job of positioning the church in the community. Nobody does an outreach event like Ed.

We do almost nothing to promote North Point Community Church in the community. We don't even have an ad in the paper. For the first year we were in our building, we didn't even have a sign out front. People in the community thought we were a doctor's office.

Our outreach is solely through word of mouth. As I explained in chapter 1, we call it our invest-and-invite strategy. We have focused the majority of our energy and resources on the Sunday morning event.

6

making membership strategic

Andy Stanley

*We make the membership process a strategic part of emphasizing
the small-group, community aspect of church.*

At the heart of any great organization or movement is a core
group of participants who eat, sleep, and dream its mission.
Ideally, in a church this core group is its members. Unfortunately,
this is not always the case—as illustrated by the large number of
churches where the membership outnumbers the attendance four
to one. At North Point Community Church, we have tried to
avoid this disconnect by making membership more strategic to
our stated mission.

We are committed to leading people into a growing relationship with Jesus Christ by creating environments where people
are encouraged and equipped to pursue intimacy with God,
community with insiders, and influence with outsiders. The
environments that we create are part of a multiple-step strategy
for moving people from the large, impersonal Sunday event to

the highly relational small group. All of our ministry efforts are designed to move an attender along this path, as I explain in more detail in later chapters. The process of membership is no different.

North Point Q & A

The first step in our strategic approach to membership is an informational luncheon called North Point Q & A. This is the only place where someone can get an application for membership. The content of this presentation is not aimed at what the church offers its members; it focuses, rather, on the mission and strategy we are asking the members to embrace. We are very clear that we are not only asking people to pursue this strategy for themselves and their friends, but also to partner with us in creating, staffing, and funding the environments necessary for its fulfillment. Our challenge to them is to either be fully on board or reconsider their decision to join North Point.

We hold this luncheon on Sunday afternoon immediately after our morning services for both convenience and in order to provide childcare. We create an environment that is not only conducive to presenting the necessary information, but that is also strategic in moving people along the spectrum of relationship that we are explaining. We put them at round tables to encourage conversation and assign them to seats based on their season of life and the area in which they live. This gives them an opportunity to meet others with whom they have a good chance of connecting relationally.

A Deeper Step

In many churches the process of membership is often handled exclusively in the large group context of the worship service. In order to make membership as strategic as possible at North Point, we have added an additional step. Instead of the prospective member turning in his or her completed application at the worship service, we require that it be taken to one of our midsized meetings, such as an Area Fellowship. There a leader must sign the application to verify that the applicant attended a smaller, more relational environment than the worship service.

This, in effect, forces all of our prospective members into the group strategy of the church. Hopefully their experience in the smaller group is of high quality, and they will want to return to it. After the application is signed, it is mailed or hand delivered to the church for processing. Then it is evaluated in light of our requirements for membership and accepted or, in some cases, delayed while we pursue further information.

The result of this strategic approach to membership is that we have a small member-to-attender ratio. However, we also have highly involved members who practice what we preach. At North Point Community Church, membership and leadership are practically synonymous.

ED'S TAKE

Imagine walking up to a professional hockey player and asking him this question: "What team do you play for?" Now suppose he answers, "I'm a professional hockey player, but I don't play for any team." You would think the guy had been slammed into the boards once too often.

A similar scenario plays out in our society when it comes to church membership. There are many people who claim to be Christ-followers, but they are not committed to a local church. I believe the Bible teaches that growing, maturing Christ-followers will be connected and committed to a local congregation. At Fellowship, membership is a high priority. It's easy to sit in the stadium and cheer for the ones on the field, but we encourage people to climb out of their seats, suit up, and play on the team called Fellowship Church.

We are up-front and honest with prospective members about who we are, where we've come from, and where we're going. And we have developed a member profile—an expectation of membership—based on that history and vision. A member must meet the following criteria: be a Christ-follower, be baptized by immersion, attend church at least three out of four weeks a month, tithe, join a small group, and participate in a ministry team. We expect people who join Fellowship to be serious about their membership. If they are not serious about their commitment to our church, then we don't want them to take up space; we encourage them to join another church where they can just sit and soak.

I have never been afraid to tell people that Fellowship Church is not for everyone—we don't even try to be. We have a unique vision that may not be shared by some people, and that's OK. We always encourage those who don't share the vision to find another church that meshes with their personalities and backgrounds.

I am also not hesitant to ask a current church member to leave Fellowship. I believe that one of the great principles of a growing church is addition by subtraction. If a church is going to grow, there are some people who need to leave. I don't mean that they are bad people; but if they don't support the values, vision, and leadership God has given us, they need to leave. Life is too short to be part of a church you don't believe in.

7

Chapter 4

closing the deal

Ed Young

*We hold a Newcomers Class to give information about the church
and prepare people to join.*

To become a member of Fellowship Church, you have to attend a Newcomers Class and then be baptized. We rarely have invitational altar calls. When I pray a salvation prayer in a service, I simply ask the people who prayed with me to check off their decision on the guest registry card and drop it in the offering plate.

The Newcomers Class is a membership class we hold every month to help people make a commitment to the Fellowship team. It is an orientation to the church and its purpose as well as a clear presentation of the gospel. Counselors follow up one-on-one to make sure everyone understands what they're doing. Following that, we offer three Fast Track classes that deal with discipleship: The Bible, The Life, and The Tithe. The Fast Track classes cover the basics of how to live and mature as a Christ-follower and how to get on the "fast track" to a successful Christian life. And then, for those who have joined the church and completed the Fast Track classes, we have a class called Discovering Your Design, which helps people find their unique, God-given gifts and teaches them how to use those gifts to serve Him.

What's Wrong with an Invitation?

Many people don't realize that walk-forward altar calls are a relatively new innovation in the Christian church. They began with the huge revivals that swept the nation in the last couple of centuries. There's no need to be attached to this particular invitational style; it is neither a biblical mandate nor something that should be set in stone.

The problem is that in the weekly church setting, an altar call can often do more harm than good. No one wants to be pointed out or recognized. A visitor to a church is almost certain to seek anonymity until they feel more comfortable, and holding an altar call is similar to asking visitors to stand up while the members remain seated.

For the first four years of Fellowship's existence, we had walk-forward invitationals every week; but the moment we switched to the Newcomers Class format, baptisms and conversions went up. We found that the class is a much less threatening and more personal environment for unchurched nonbelievers to explore the meaning of Christianity.

Besides, anything that you do week after week becomes boring and eventually loses its meaning. Having a Newcomers

Class keeps us from depending every week on a routine invitational that has lost its punch. We do still, on occasion, have altar calls, because we understand that some people need that extra prodding to walk up the aisle and make a decision for Christ. These invitationals have been very well received, but they are not our norm.

How Does It Work?

The Newcomers Class is offered each month at three different times: after a Saturday night service, after the Sunday morning services, and on a Thursday night. Dinner and childcare are always provided. Tracy Barnes, our Pastor of Assimilation who is in charge of the membership process, leads each class.

Tracy begins with an explanation of our vision statement: "Fellowship Church exists to reach up in worship, to reach out in evangelism, and to reach in in discipleship." The concept of reaching up leads right into the salvation message. If visitors have only attended Fellowship a few times before deciding to join, they may never have heard how to have a personal relationship with Jesus. Tracy explains the salvation message and prays the sinner's prayer with them. We don't want people to slip through the cracks and become members without ever making the decision to trust Christ with their lives.

Tracy also discusses baptism and communion, explaining that baptism is also required for membership. He goes through evangelism and discipleship and closes with a discussion of our church structure. This is when he explains that Fellowship is a member of the Southern Baptist Convention and a staff-led church.

At the end of this presentation, which lasts forty-five minutes to an hour, everyone has three choices. If they want to join the church, they stay seated. If they just aren't ready at that moment, they can leave and join later when they're sure that's what they want to do. The third option is to leave and find another church. We explain that our church isn't the church for everyone and that our prayer is that they get involved *somewhere*. There's plenty of moving around at this time, so the ones who leave aren't made to feel conspicuous.

Usually 90 to 95 percent of the people stay, and the other 5 percent almost always join later. From the three classes, about 200 to 250 people join our church each month. Trained counselors spend about fifteen to twenty minutes with each person or couple, helping them to fill out membership cards that include, along with their name, address, and other demographic information, a place to indicate their personal testimony and what ministries they're interested in. If it looks like they're still unsure of what it means to be a Christian, the counselor will walk them through the salvation message a second time and even pray with them again, if necessary.

A table for baptism sign-up is right there as people finish talking with their counselors. If they've just been saved or have never been baptized by immersion, they can sign up that day. We also have a table to register for the Fast Track classes, which is the next step for new members. Photographers are available outside so we can have pictures of all our members on file.

Church membership is not—and we emphasize this—a requirement for salvation. But it is an important step toward service and involvement in the ministry of a local body of believers. It's a serious step, indicating a readiness to be plugged into the life of the church, but it should also be a painless and even pleasant process. How you welcome new members into the church says a lot about how you will care for them over the long run.

ANDY'S TAKE

The difference between what Ed and I do as it relates to membership can probably be summarized this way: We focus on a process, whereas Ed focuses on content. As you know from reading the previous chapter, North Point doesn't have a class for new members. Instead, we have four steps that candidates must complete before joining. Our goal in the membership process is to move people one step closer to community. Ed's goal is to inform candidates about what it means to be a member of Fellowship Church.

Which way is better? Well, Ed has 150 to 200 new members each month. We average around fifty. Go, Ed!

section **2**

ministering to people

8

kidstuf

Andy Stanley

We provide a place where kids take their parents to learn.

Most conventional models of church tend to segregate the family. Parents and children usually go in separate directions when they arrive on the church grounds. Sundays are rarely a shared experience for the family.

The exception is in churches where children are expected to attend adult worship services with their parents. But putting kids in an adult environment to get them inspired about what their parents believe is sometimes counterproductive. Elementary-aged children can easily become programmed to switch off their minds a few minutes into the service. There is also a tendency for a bored child to become a distraction to parents, as well as to other adults.

So why not reverse the concept? Instead of putting kids in an adult world, why not put parents in a kid's world? At North

Point we have discovered that it's a lot easier to get parents excited about learning something with their kids than it is to get kids excited about sitting in an environment designed for adults. So every Sunday following adult worship, our grade school children and their parents come together for a unique, forty-five minute experience designed to communicate biblical truth to the entire family.

Family-Centered

At North Point KidStuf is not a children's church. It's a "family-centered" ministry that requires parental involvement. By creating an environment for parents and kids to attend together, KidStuf serves as a catalyst for the parent/child relationship. We have discovered that a number of families are so busy during the week that they are looking for things to do with their kids on the weekend. By making KidStuf a priority, our church has made an important statement about the family as a unit.

Every week KidStuf reminds families that the children's ministry doesn't exist as a substitute for parenting, but rather to complement parenting. At every age level, we want to make sure parents never have the attitude, "I'm going to drop off my kids and hope the church can fix them spiritually or morally." KidStuf encourages parents to spend quality time and assume the role of spiritual leaders with their children.

Kid-Focused

KidStuf is an upbeat environment for elementary-aged children designed to make learning both fun and relevant. A percentage of the production strives to relate to a range of age levels. We call this our "Lion King" approach to ministry. At times the humor and dialogue directly target adults, and at other moments the message is geared for younger children. The greatest portion of the production, however, is aimed at fourth and fifth graders. We have discovered that if we successfully connect with the older kids, we still keep the younger audience engaged. We allow the older kids to assume various roles of leadership and participate with our adult and teenage singers, so the production has an older elementary-aged feel.

Values-Driven

At KidStuf a core value, along with a simple definition of that value, is displayed onstage and becomes the bottom line for an entire month of programs. Since values influence behavior and determine what is viewed as important in life, we have a three-year calendar that revolves around thirty-six values that are significant for every family. The meaning of each value is taught through examples from the Bible, nature, object lessons, and skits depicting everyday life. Occasionally supplemental materials are provided to help families reinforce and apply the values at home.

Creatively Wired

We found that one of the most important things to do when trying to create a relevant environment for children is to learn from the experts. Instead of asking other churches what they were doing for their kids, we took our cue from organizations like Nickelodeon and Disney. Over the course of forty-five minutes, we use storytelling, skits, videos, activities, and music designed to both entertain and teach families. A creative team meets each week to plan the twelve segments that make up a typical production. We also have a Web site (www.kidstuf.com) where families can participate and respond to various KidStuf issues.

User-Friendly

The primary marketing tool for promoting KidStuf is word of mouth. Regular attenders know they can invite other families to come to KidStuf and be confident they will have a predictable, quality experience. KidStuf has become a great entry point for unchurched families. We strive to keep the style and message of the production nonthreatening, so we can continue to be effective in reaching families who are normally not interested in church. We provide gift bags for visiting families that include an introduction to our adult worship services and Area Fellowships. This helps create an awareness for newcomers of other programs that are available for their family members. Each week KidStuf averages about thirty families who are visiting North Point for the first time. A large percentage of those who initially meet us through KidStuf end up considering us their church.

Volunteer-Fueled

KidStuf is definitely a team effort. Nearly twenty teams of almost two hundred people make the productions successful. KidStuf parents are invited to participate by helping each week or month with the registration, resources, creative, host, production, and technical teams. By providing a variety of low-key volunteer options, every parent can find something to do to help. In fact, it is not unusual for unchurched parents to volunteer. As a result many of these "outsiders" develop a relationship with seasoned leaders who ultimately help them connect with the adult ministries of our church.

Any Objections?

KidStuf is without question a shift away from most conventional children's ministries. Those who visit us from other churches occasionally question the idea of parents attending a children's program. Many are accustomed to handing their children off to volunteers or teachers so they can go on to adult Sunday school. And in some churches, the worship staff would feel threatened by an event on campus that drew adults away from "big church." Sometimes it has been easier for unchurched or nontraditional parents to grasp the concept. The reason

KidStuf works at North Point is because we have a passion for reaching unchurched families, and we want parents to be partners with us when it comes to teaching their children about faith and character.

(For more information about how to do KidStuf in your church, contact us through our Web site at www.KidStuf.com.)

ED'S TAKE

KidStuf is one of the most creative concepts in children's ministry in America. I applaud the creativity of Andy and the North Point staff for reaching the unchurched with this great idea. If you have multiple services, one logistical concern that would need to be worked out to implement this kind of program is the traffic congestion between services. Traffic buildup is a major deterrent to newcomers, so you need to be careful that this combined parent/child service does not prevent a smooth transition.

No matter what kind of children's ministry your church does, it has to be done with excellence. If you can reach the kids, you will reach the parents. When we rank our priorities at Fellowship, children always come before adults. We spend money, build space, and provide resources for our children's ministry because it is so important to the future of the church. I hear story after story of children being dropped off to attend our children's programs and loving them so much that it leads to their parents' regular attendance and involvement in the church.

If you are trying to start or grow a church, your children's ministry has to be a top priority. Are the facilities modern and clean? Are the workers competent, and have they been thoroughly screened? Is there adequate security? Is the Bible study relevant and age appropriate? Do parents trust you with their kids? If they don't, they won't come back. In today's culture, parents are very particular about the safety and well-being of their children.

Our children's church, Adventure World, is a microcosm of our adult worship services. We use drama, games, puppets, video, contemporary music, and applicable teaching in our kids' services. We also include special events such as summer camps, basketball leagues, and vacation Bible school.

Kids Just Wanna Have Fun!

Adventure World serves a dual purpose in the life of Fellowship Church. The first purpose is for children two years old through fifth grade to hear and experience the life-changing principles of the Bible. The second is for the kids to have *fun!* We believe that when kids are having fun, they are actively engaged in the lesson; when they are actively engaged in the lesson, they are learning; and when they are learning, they are growing. Every event that is planned—from summer camp to

Adventure Week to Adventure World Weekends—is structured with these two principles in mind.

Adventure World's goal is to give this generation of kids a positive view of the local church. Too often we hear that church is boring. If that is true, then the church will become irrelevant; and if the church becomes irrelevant, then children will quit coming as soon as they are allowed to. Children should leave church smiling from ear to ear and asking the question, "When can we come back?" Here's how we try to make it happen at Fellowship Church.

Adventure World Weekends

Every weekend during the adult worship services, we have Adventure World Weekends for kids four years old through fifth grade. These fun programs are age appropriate and packed with excitement. Here are some key concepts we employ:

Fun Is the Word

For Adventure World Weekends, *fun* is the operative word. Activities are designed to teach as well as to entertain. Eighty percent of what takes place in the program is intended to focus kids toward the main point of the day. But sometimes the sole function of a particular activity is simply to allow the children to have fun and enjoy being kids. If kids have fun, they will want to come back; and if they come back, they will learn about the Bible and develop a positive, lifelong attitude toward the local church.

All Kids Allowed

During Adventure World Weekends, we take into special consideration the child who knows nothing about the Bible. Our goal is to have everyone feel included and part of the action whether they know a lot, a little, or nothing at all about what the Bible says. Activities that call for Bible knowledge simply review what has been learned that day, thus giving the excitement of knowing the right answer to all the children.

Learning Level

Because kids are able to learn different things at different age levels, we gear our programming specifically toward different age groups. Too often, when kids from kindergarten through fifth grade are placed in a learning environment together, the older kids begin to feel that the material presented, no matter how great it is, is not for them. This leads to a perception that the teaching time is "for babies," and the older kids tune out. At Adventure World Weekends, we break our kids into three levels: four and five year olds, kindergarten through second grade, and third through fifth grade. This allows us to focus our teaching and creativity according to the learning ability of each group.

The Wow Factor

When time and effort are put into designing the place where kids are going to be learning, the kids sense that, and it adds to their enthusiasm level. We take our teaching environment very seriously. We want the environment of an Adventure World Weekend to shout, "Wow! This is fun!" Something we've found useful is a large, fifty-four-inch-wide, full-color print plotter that helps us make great backdrops quickly and easily.

Life Impact

Small groups are critical for making an Adventure World Weekend a true success. Often when kids are brought into a large children's church, they have very little one-on-one interaction with an adult. In Adventure World we have adult leaders who commit to leading small groups of kids during a special breakout session. In these small groups, the kids are helped to understand the life application of the lesson that is being taught that day. These same small-group leaders are also challenged to maintain contact with the families of the children in their group beyond the confines of the church itself.

Apply It

The Internet is a key in helping kids remember what they learn each weekend. Every week a quiz is placed on-line that asks eight to ten questions related to the previous Adventure

World Weekend's service. If kids get all the answers correct, they receive a prize the next weekend. This encourages the children to strive to remember what they learn and reintroduces them to the lesson during the week.

Family Ties

We encourage parents to participate as small-group leaders in Adventure World Weekends. This affords the family an opportunity to experience the spiritual connectedness of attending church together. Having parents serve also gives them the opportunity to understand the message being taught to their children, so they can review it with their kids throughout the week. For those parents not able to be involved in Adventure World, we provide a "Parents Letter" that describes what happened during the service and gives them points to review with their children during the week.

Summertime Action

What a great time summer is for really getting into a kid's life! So often churches try to make an impact on children by focusing solely on the weekend worship services. At Adventure World we take full advantage of the extra time the kids have in the summer by providing activities that allow us to get more deeply into their lives. Two major programs that help us do that are Summer Extreme and Adventure Week.

Summer Extreme

This is a week-long event in which kids get away and immerse themselves twenty-four hours a day in fun activities, lessons, and Extreme Nights, a Nickelodeon-type program that presents a biblical message in a dynamic way and encourages full participation. During the week the children are constantly surrounded by adults and youth who love Christ. This opens up a realm of interaction that can only happen over an extended time period.

Adventure Week

This is an all-out nightly program running Monday through Friday that includes:

- A high-octane, half-hour drama containing music, laughter, audience participation, and a presentation of the main point for the evening

- Activities in which kids can participate according to their age group—designed to allow each child to have the maximum amount of fun

- A study time involving drama, puppets, music, and illustrations in which the kids are once again presented with the main point of the evening, with a focus on life application

Summer Extreme and Adventure Week are only two of our programs that involve kids outside the typical Saturday/Sunday service structure. In Adventure World, we want children to understand that being a Christ-follower is a twenty-four-hour, seven-days-a-week thing. Activities apart from our weekend services—when we can have a child's attention for three or more hours at a time—help us in achieving this goal.

Salvation for Kids

Children coming to know Christ as their personal Savior is the greatest thing that can happen within a children's ministry. In Adventure World, we get the parents involved in their children's salvation decision whenever possible. On a regular basis (at least six times a year) the life-changing message of Christ is presented. If any children make a decision for Christ, their parents are contacted and invited to attend a class entitled KidFaith. Everything the kids have been taught about Christ is presented again to the parents and the kids. Attending KidFaith gives parents the opportunity to be involved in their children's decision to accept Christ. Then, as the children grow up, the parents can remind them of the time they made their faith decision, easing the doubts that so often come to children about their salvation.

Overall, our goal is simple: Get kids and their families involved in the local church by providing excellent and creative programs in which they can have fun and learn about God. If kids come back with a smile on their face, we know we are doing something right.

(For more information about Adventure World for Kids or any of our other programs, be sure to attend our annual Creative Church Conference for pastors and church leaders held every January at Fellowship Church. Detailed information is available at www.fellowshipchurch.com.)

aligning student ministry

Andy Stanley

We understand and plan for the unique relational and ministry needs of junior high and high school students.

The traditional approach to student ministry is to replicate the Sunday morning small group or classroom model used in the preschool and children's ministries. At North Point Community Church, we have chosen instead to align our high school ministry with our adult ministries.

The overall mission of North Point Community Church is to lead people into a growing relationship with Jesus Christ, emphasizing three vital relationships: with God, with insiders, and with outsiders. Further, we have identified three key environments in which to develop these relationships. We refer to these environments as the Foyer, the Living Room, and the Kitchen.

Likewise, our student ministry mission is to lead people into a growing relationship with Jesus Christ by creating environments in which students can prioritize their relationship with

Christ, influence their friends, and experience personal ministry. The three key environments are created with a uniquely student-centered feel to effectively carry out our mission statement.

The Foyer

North Point defines the Foyer as an entry point, like the entry to your home—a place for guests. We have created student environments with this focus in mind. The Zone, for middle school students, takes place the last Sunday of each month and plans with the guest in mind. Students are encouraged to bring their lost or unchurched friends. The program is fun and upbeat with a live band, skits, and games. It encourages interaction among the students. The gospel is presented each time, and students are encouraged to take the next step, which in this case is moving to the teaching environment (called Xtreme).

Rush Hour is a monthly event created to provide a first step into the church for high school students. It focuses on the unbeliever or the unchurched and is a step toward the small-group, discipleship environment (InsideOut).

The Living Room

North Point defines the Living Room as a place where you make friends. Xtreme, for middle schoolers, provides a great place on Sunday mornings for friends to gather with each other. This is where the concept of small groups is introduced, and leaders are encouraged to develop a sense of friendship that includes accountability and prayer. Xtreme provides a good transition into the high school ministry and InsideOut.

The Kitchen

The kitchen is identified as a place for family (think of sitting around the kitchen table). Every step in our church is designed to lead people to the small-group environment of the kitchen table. Small groups are where we believe real life change takes place.

InsideOut is designed for high school students who want to make their relationship with Christ a priority. This is the place where they gather on Sunday afternoons for worship and praise, teaching, and small-group interaction. The dynamic of the group encourages accountability, spiritual application, prayer, and relationships.

Strategic Service

North Point Community Church has a very unique perspective when it comes to membership. Each member of North Point is asked to serve in some capacity. We believe in this so strongly that we do not provide Sunday school for adults (married or single) on Sunday mornings. Instead, adults are encouraged to attend worship one hour and serve in some capacity the other hour.

We believe that each student is uniquely gifted and has a

responsibility to serve as well. The Student Impact program allows high school students to participate in strategic service and experience personal ministry. Students are encouraged to attend worship one hour and serve the other hour alongside the adults of our church.

ED'S TAKE

Edge Student Ministry of Fellowship Church strives to be a place where kids who know Christ can experience intense worship and relevant Bible study. But it is equally a place where they can invite their lost friends, knowing that they will enjoy a generationally targeted, life-changing program—a program they can be proud of.

Junior High Ministries

Wild Side (Large Group Time)

Wild Side meets on Wednesday nights and has two main purposes. The first is for our students to be able to bring their friends into an exciting atmosphere where they can be introduced to Christ. The second is for our students to gain biblical truth to help them live out their faith in their families, in their neighborhoods, and on their campuses.

During each Wild Side session, we strive to drive home one biblical point during our twelve to fifteen-minute speaking time using themed series; stage props; crowd interaction;

upbeat and intense worship music; videos; and relevant, junior high-specific teaching. We strive for excellence from the moment the students walk in the door.

Wild Side meets year round, including the summer. We take only three nights off for holidays.

Grade Meetings (Medium Group Time)

Following the Wild Side time, our students meet in their grade rooms. All sixth, seventh, and eighth grade students meet in three separate rooms with their grade pastor for the medium group time of the evening. This portion is designed for the grade pastor to make a connection with the students by giving announcements that pertain not only to Wild Side in general, but also to their grade specifically. During this time students officially take roll so that we have a 100 percent accurate attendance count, which is used for that week's follow-up on absentees. These records are also used to track student attendance within that calendar year and the years to follow so that growth patterns can be charted.

Family Groups (Small Group Time)

Our Family Group time is designed to do three things. First, it is a final opportunity to drive home the one main point for the evening through a scripture verse and five or six questions that each small group's "trainer" uses during the discussion time. Second, it allows students to build new relationships with other students who more than likely attend their campus. And third, it gives the trainers a chance to build relationships with the students they will be ministering to during the entire school year. It is each leader's responsibility to not only lead the group for the evening but also to get into the students' lives by attending activities and events with them, ministering to them one-on-one outside of the Wednesday night format, and contacting them when they are absent.

Access (Discipleship)

Access is our junior high discipleship ministry. It's designed to take students through five specific five-week courses over their three years in our junior high program. It also includes four elective classes (a divorce recovery class, a climbing class, a career class, and a student/parent relationship class) using a variety of formats. This area of ministry is user-friendly to all students, no matter the level of their personal Christian growth. It also offers students a more intensive and directed praise and worship time.

We also provide two classes for parents. One is eight weeks long and deals specifically with parenting issues (communication, discipline, student needs, etc.). The other is a three-week course on preparing for and dealing with a child's dating life. All classes are directed by our discipleship pastor, who also compiles and/or writes all materials.

Special Events (Outreach)

Special events are intended to impact students and families in a way that will interest them in getting actively and regularly involved in our student ministry. For example, first-time visitors to Wild Side receive staked signs on the front lawn of their homes thanking them for visiting with us. Attached to the signs are letters to the parents thanking them for allowing their students to attend, inviting them to visit Fellowship Church, and then giving general church information for the entire family. The signs also have letters to the students and coupons to be traded in at the student ministry café for a free item for them and any friends they bring with them the next time they visit. These signs are placed in the yards while the students are at Wild Side, so they see them upon arriving home that evening.

Various mission projects are offered to give students the opportunity to serve others, to develop leadership qualities, and to allow them to make a broader impact in the world. In the summer we offer a camp called Beach Retreat designed to draw unsaved and unchurched students. The sole purpose of this retreat is to reach students with the good news of Christ and then encourage them and their families to become active in Fellowship Church.

We offer a unique program to the local schools—a two-hour climbing and teamwork session on our very own climbing wall. The session is free of charge for teacher groups, school staffs, and student sports teams. This gets students and teachers onto our campus and allows us to develop relationships with school administrations. Our staff members are on school campuses weekly for lunch, and they also attend sporting events in order to spend time with students on their turf.

Senior High Ministries

The Mix (Large Group Time)

The Mix meets on Wednesday nights and draws students from various backgrounds across the area (the name refers to the mix of students we have each Wednesday night). Through different mediums, students recognize their need for God and experience the relevancy of God for their lives. Its purpose is threefold: To serve as a weekly outreach event in which our core students invite their friends; to communicate in creative, cutting-edge ways the life-changing message of Jesus Christ; and to provide a place where students can safely build lasting relationships.

The Mix is designed to be a place where trust exists and ownership of the night belongs to the students. Creating such a place requires several things: student involvement in weekly programming, a clear picture of the purpose of the program, and a team that will raise the bar of excellence in every element of the program. Because of the ownership the students have, as well as the trust we have built with them by stressing excellence, they are excited about coming and bringing their friends.

Each Wednesday the program points to "one thing"—for example, God's desire for a teenager's dating life. Students see this "one thing" through video, feel it through music, and hear it through a message tailor-made for them. Packaged strategically and intentionally, the Mix is never the same from week to week. We change our programming frequently to keep students intrigued and guessing.

Campus Teams (Medium Group Time)

Each Wednesday night before The Mix, our students meet in campus teams. These teams are made up of students from specific schools within a region of the Dallas/Fort Worth area. On any given night, we have some thirty-five-plus high schools represented in five campus teams. Campus teams serve as a relational base for student before going to the Mix. The teams give students an opportunity to meet and make new friends that go to their school or live in their region. Campus teams also provide students with a place to build unity and be strategic about reaching their campuses for Christ.

Campus teams are directed by a campus team coordinator who serves as the pastor for their schools. The coordinators are responsible for the leadership within their campus teams and serve as a relational connection to the ministry. Campus team coordinators are assisted by three campus team captains—students who have displayed leadership within their schools and live a

Christ-filled life of integrity. This is another way of giving more ownership of the student ministry to students.

Fe Groups (Small Group Time)

A great large group program is not enough. Students need a relational connection. Without people to step in and "do life" with our students, our program is a failure. That is why we do Fe Groups, which meet weekly following the Mix. *Fe* is the chemical symbol for iron, and these groups provide "iron sharpening iron" relationships. Students, led by their small-group trainers, are challenged to find personal application for the evening's "one thing."

The Foundry (Discipleship)

After students have experienced life change, we encourage them to take the next step in their walk with God: discipleship. The Foundry meets weekly on Sunday nights at 6 P.M. Through the Foundry, students experience authentic worship and have the opportunity to pick one of eight classes, ranging from the basics of Christianity to apologetics. Students are challenged to share what they learn with their friends. The Foundry serves as an equipping time to get students involved in the leadership of the student ministry and the church as a whole.

At the Foundry students can also be a part of the League, a service ministry made up of nine ministry teams. These teams give students the opportunity to serve within the other ministries of the church, thereby living out the last part of Fellowship's vision statement: to *reach in* through discipleship.

Special Events (Outreach)

When students in our community hear the word *church,* we want them to think *Fellowship Church.* We want them to know that at Fellowship Church we genuinely care about them. In order to accomplish this, we strategically plan outreach events. Students are not going to just show up at our door. We must do as Christ did and reach out to them.

We are extremely intentional and strategic about letting students know that we want to do more than just give them instruction. We desire to reach out to them and then walk alongside them through their high school years. We accomplish this through weekly lunch visits by staff and volunteers, tailgate parties during football season, and staff attendance at other school events.

The school year is the busiest time for the senior high ministries. But during the summer, we stay involved in our students' lives through camps and the Mix. There is no break in student ministry. God has given us an urgent call to reach this generation, and that is a daily task.

The students have a saying around Fellowship Church: "No one does events like Fellowship." We are proud of that reputation. Students know through our camps, outreach events, and weekly programming—all done with excellence—that we care for them. That attitude has gained our students' trust. And with that trust, we are reaching and will continue to reach hundreds and thousands of high school students across the Dallas/Fort Worth area.

10

welcome teams

Ed Young

*We have four distinct teams that focus on
specific areas of weekend hospitality.*

At Fellowship Church we have four teams that serve and
welcome people to our church: parkers, greeters, hospitality
booth workers, and ushers. Parkers wearing orange vests are
strategically placed out in the parking lot, directing people to
the closest parking spots and to the church entrances. Greeters
are stationed at the entrances, welcoming everyone who enters.
The hospitality booth, which serves free bagels, donuts, and
Starbucks coffee, is located in our atrium. Finally, multitudes of
ushers stand in our worship center, passing out programs at the
door and directing people to seats.

We believe the first impression a visitor gets is invaluable.
The volunteers on all four of these teams are always smiling and
cheerful. Their goal is to make visitors, as well as regular attendees, feel at ease and welcome (without overdoing it).

Obviously, providing free food is expensive, but it's worth it. We get many, many comments on how wonderful the hospitality booth is. While free coffee by itself may not attract people to the church, it is a step beyond anything a visitor expects. It impresses people, and they see our sincerity and commitment to service.

Making It Work

You must be a member to serve in any capacity at Fellowship Church, but becoming a member is not difficult to do (see chapter 7, "Closing the Deal"). At our Newcomers Class, we immediately give new members the opportunity to sign up for more information about ministries that they'd like to be involved in. At Fellowship we have places for everyone to serve—men and women, single and married, young and old. Many new members choose to get involved in welcome teams because these ministries are low commitment, easy, and nonthreatening. We've found that getting them on a team prevents them from coming in the front door and going out the back; if they're involved in a ministry from the beginning, they're much less likely to fade away and never do anything.

Our church also has an information booth with brochures telling about the different welcome ministries, so anyone in the church can find out how to sign up. Once members indicate interest in one of the four welcome areas, we call them to explain the purpose of the ministry and how it works. We schedule them to start on the day when we need the most people and tell them where to sign in. For the first few weeks, they get paired up with seasoned buddies who can show them the ropes.

For the greeters, for example, the goal is to make sure that not one person walks through the door without being welcomed. The greeters offer help if someone looks lost and give information on childcare, Bible study classes, the bookstore, and so on. If someone happens to ask a question that the greeter can't answer, that person is directed to the information booth.

The welcome teams arrive forty-five minutes before a service begins and stay at their posts until at least fifteen minutes after it starts. It's usually best that they not try to attend the same service in which they serve. With four service times, they can easily volunteer in one service and attend another. There are at least 450 parkers and 250 people in hospitality and greeting. They are on a three-week rotation, meaning that they serve one week and are off two. We try to dissuade people from doubling up in two different ministry areas; if everyone is serving in an area, then no one should need to serve in two.

For a church our size, the parking ministry, in particular, takes a tremendous amount of coordination. But without the dedicated individuals who serve as parkers, our parking lots would be in a state of chaos every weekend. And there is no quicker way to turn off a visitor than for the parking situation to be a nightmare. Our parking team has three chairpersons to oversee the ministry and coordinate all of the logistical ins and outs. Their planning strategies keep traffic flowing and get people in parking spots as quickly and efficiently as possible. Each chairperson oversees several shift captains, who are responsible for the various weekend services and for calling volunteers to remind them of their responsibilities.

The welcome teams may be easy, low-commitment ministries, but they are high-impact. Except for the weekend messages, more people are impacted by these greeting and hospitality teams than by any other ministry in the church. First impressions are so important. If people feel welcome at Fellowship Church from the start, we know they are likely to come back.

The Camaraderie of Ministry

Often the loneliest people in the church are those who are not serving in ministry. Our welcome team members become connected not only with the church as a whole, but also with each other as a family. Not long ago one of the guys in our parking ministry lost his home to a fire. He had three kids, not enough insurance to cover the damage, and was in real need of help. The other volunteers in the parking ministry heard about this family's need and took up a collection for several weeks to help get them back on their feet again. This is what the ministry of the church is all about: people caring for people. And when we get people involved in ministry from the very beginning, they not only have an opportunity to meet the needs of others, but they also have their own needs met along the way.

ANDY'S TAKE

At North Point we have eight Host teams. Each team consists of about one hundred members and is scheduled to work one service per month, allowing even busy people to get involved.

We do not require Host team members to be church members. In fact, we don't even require them to be believers. Just about every Host team has seekers who are part of the group. This is intentional; we've found that for many seekers, community is the door to conversion. Is it risky having seekers and nonmembers involved in this way? Yes. But we think the evangelistic upside makes it well worth it.

11

community groups

Andy Stanley

We emphasize small groups as a place to find real community.

Success at North Point Community Church is defined by how effectively our ministries move people from our larger group environments to North Point's version of the small group, which we call a community group. We believe a community group is the best place for sustained life change to occur. Practically speaking, there will never be a way for the church staff or elders to personally minister to everyone who attends our church. That's why we place such a high premium on small-group life. It's how we minister effectively.

The goal of a North Point community group is to provide a predictable environment where people can experience authentic community and spiritual growth. Made up of four to six couples or five to eight individuals, a community group is the place where people are personally encouraged and challenged in their relationship with God and with each other. Not only is it a perfect setting for studying God's Word, it's a personal enough environment to tackle the tough questions and challenges in people's lives. And it's a place where they can pray for one another and care for one another. In a community group, they're missed if they don't show up.

Team Structure

There are four key players in the community group leadership structure: the assimilator, the group leader, the coach, and the group director. The *assimilator* is responsible for creating environments that move worship service and area fellowship attenders into community groups. The *group leader* is responsible for shepherding the group and facilitating the actual group meeting. As a result, he or she is the most important person in the group process.

The *coach* is responsible for leading and developing up to five group leaders and monitoring the health and effectiveness of each group. The *group director* is a staff person responsible for leading and developing twelve to fifteen coaches. This person also plays a strategic role in the interview process for new coaches and leaders.

Leadership Training

Since our strategy for growth is primarily based on multiplication, every leader and coach is expected to have an apprentice. An apprentice is not someone who simply assists a group leader;

rather, he or she is someone who has the potential and passion to lead and shepherd a community group. We believe apprenticing is the most effective way to train new group leaders.

In addition to the apprenticing process, our leadership training includes:

- A leaders' orientation for new group leaders and coaches twice a year

- A retreat for all leaders, coaches, and apprentices each fall

- Spring mini-retreats for each season-of-life division (married groups, singles groups, etc.)

- Quarterly meetings between coaches and their leaders, both individually and as a group

- Biweekly "leadership tips" sent to all leaders and coaches

Covenant Relationships

We believe that predictability is a critical component for building authentic community. Relationships take time to develop, and group environments that constantly change work against this process. As a result, community groups are closed groups; no additional members are added during its duration unless all of the group members agree. The groups meet for twelve to eighteen months and then multiply into one or more new groups.

Each community group makes a covenant, which is a tool to manage group life and establish expectations. When expectations are not defined, frustration always follows. While the group leader plays an important role in guiding this process, each group determines when they meet, how long they meet, and what curriculum they will study. The group also determines through the covenant how time is spent in the actual meeting (for example, how much time is devoted to fellowship, sharing, study, and prayer).

Group Vision

At North Point we are committed to reducing the obstacles that keep people from getting into community. And since childcare expenses can be one of the biggest roadblocks to participation in a small group, we reimburse members at a prescribed rate for the childcare expenses incurred while attending their community group. Our vision is for 80 percent of our attenders to be in some kind of small-group environment by 2004. Small-group life, we're convinced, is the key to our mission of leading people into a growing relationship with Jesus Christ.

ED'S TAKE

Small groups are a vital part of the community experience at Fellowship Church. When I have the opportunity, I talk about the biblical principle of small groups during my messages. I lead a small group, as does every one of our program and management staff members. From time to time we may devote an entire weekend to emphasizing the importance of becoming involved in a small group.

Since the beginning of Fellowship Church, we have delegated ministry to the members of the church. Ministry always works better one-on-one. There is no way our staff can meet all of the needs of our congregation. We rely on our small group ministry to be the first line of care when someone needs help. I am always amazed at how quickly small groups show up at the hospital, provide meals, and meet the needs of families who are hurting.

We divide our small-group program into three types of groups.

HomeTeams

These are groups of married or single adults who meet in homes across the Dallas/Fort Worth area at least twice a month. They are led by a "builder" and an "apprentice builder," with a "developer" providing support, encouragement, and accountability for four to five builders and groups. HomeTeams are always open to visitors, because we encourage our participants to bring their friends and neighbors to the meetings. Each group is responsible for its own childcare.

All HomeTeams use the same study material. Because we believe that every activity should mirror the purposes of the church, we select studies built around our purpose statement. For the first four months of the year, we do a study on our first purpose of "reaching up," or worship. Over the next four months, we select a study on "reaching out," or evangelism. During the last four months, we do a study on "reaching in," or discipleship. This schedule allows us to continually teach our purpose statement to our congregation. I hesitate to allow groups to select their own material because there are so many studies available that appear to be biblical but are not. My goal is to eventually publish our own small-group material.

We hold monthly training sessions for new builders and apprentices. We also provide training via our Web site and hold quarterly training rallies for all HomeTeam leadership. The rallies are a great time of celebration, testimonies, and vision casting for the small-group ministry. Leadership training is also accomplished as apprentice builders receive on-the-job training and guidance from builders and developers.

Common Ground Teams

These are groups of people who meet based on a common experience—for example, groups for newly married or engaged couples, new believer groups, men's and women's groups, financial freedom groups, athletic teams, and support and recovery groups. The Common Ground Teams meet for eight to twelve sessions and are usually closed because of the short, intense study time. Group locations vary depending on the study. Some of the groups meet on campus, while others meet off campus. We cycle these groups at least three times a year.

Task Teams

These are groups of people who share a common ministry task. They include preschool and children's workers, youth leaders, ushers, greeters, the praise team, the drama team, and so on. The Task Teams usually meet on campus before or after the participants complete their ministry task. The meeting is a shortened version of a HomeTeam or Common Ground meeting, but that time is just as meaningful for the participants.

Basically we try to build small groups into every Bible study we have at Fellowship. Our preschool, children's, and student ministries utilize small groups to build relationships and talk about biblical principles. Every adult Bible study class during the week or on the weekends has a small-group time in which participants can meet other people, talk about the application of the lesson, and pray together. Each group has a trained leader who is responsible for group discussion, prayer time, and keeping in touch with group members during the week.

12

area fellowships

Andy Stanley

*We utilize Area Fellowships to get people
to begin to connect relationally.*

One of the challenges facing a growing church is how to transition people from the large-group environment of the worship service to the small-group environment of a small group— or as we say at North Point, from the foyer to the kitchen. We designed Area Fellowships as a bridge to facilitate the move from the large group to a small group, from our worship services to our small community group meetings. For the average worship service attender, an Area Fellowship is the next step of involvement.

Descriptions and Definitions

The goal of our Area Fellowships is to create a fun environment where people can begin to connect relationally. These are not Bible studies. If you are familiar with the adult Sunday school model, think of an Area Fellowship as the opening assembly before class.

Area Fellowships are organized according to two criteria: location and stage of life. They meet on the first weekend of every month in homes, clubhouses, backyards, and parks, with catered dinners built around a theme. They are open to anyone who wishes to attend and range in size from forty to about eighty people. Typically, one-third of those who attend are first-time visitors to the Area Fellowship; another third are already participating in a small group; and the remaining third is waiting to be assimilated into a small group. In this way the Area Fellowship serves as a "waiting room" for those who have not yet connected with a small group.

The Event

In addition to eating and having fun, each Area Fellowship event includes a time when the coordinator recasts North Point's small-group vision and explains the relationship between the Area Fellowship and a community group. From time to time individuals or couples will share testimonies about something meaningful that has happened in their small groups.

Toward the end of the evening, the group coordinator asks for a show of hands of those who are already in a community group. Then they will ask those who are interested in joining a group to identify themselves. Those who indicate a desire to join a small group are then encouraged to sign up for Group Link, an event designed to introduce people to group life.

Leadership Positions

There are three leadership positions associated with each Area Fellowship: the group coordinator, the assimilator, and the coach. Depending upon the size of the group, there may be more than one assimilator and coach.

The group coordinator is responsible for scheduling and planning the monthly event. Generally, he or she forms a team to help with this responsibility. The assimilator's responsibility is to network and introduce couples to each other with the goal of forming new community groups. The coach is responsible for monitoring existing community groups and coaching group leaders. (For more information on Area Fellowships, please visit our Web site at www.northpoint.org.)

ED'S TAKE

At Fellowship we bridge the gap between the large (celebration) group and the small (cell) group through medium-sized groups that meet in Power Source studies, Connection classes, and HomeTeam Open House receptions. Power Source studies are Bible studies held during the week on the church campus. Connection classes are age-group based Bible study classes held on campus before or after weekend worship services. In a

Connection class, a master teacher leads a group of 50 to 250 attendees through a Bible study and then into small-group breakout sessions. We call these Connection classes because the connections people make to God's Word bring about exciting life changes, and the connections they make with other believers often lead to their involvement in HomeTeams.

This year we will begin hosting HomeTeam Open House receptions designed to welcome new participants into existing HomeTeams. They will be held on site and will be catered with snacks and beverages. Our goal is for the receptions to be places for current builders, HomeTeam leaders, and group members to meet interested parties from their area and invite them to their groups.

13

group link
Andy Stanley

*We move people from Area Fellowships to Group Link,
an environment designed to jump-start small groups.*

One of the biggest challenges facing a church committed to involving people in small groups is the process of connecting people. For a small group to work, there must be a certain level of chemistry among the participants. This is why assigning adults to groups generally doesn't work.

As I noted in the previous chapter, at North Point Community Church the primary environment from which small groups are formed is the Area Fellowship. Ideally, individuals or couples will attend their monthly Area Fellowship meeting and over time be invited to join a community group that is looking for new members. The advantage to this system is that it allows people to gravitate relationally into our small-group ministry. The disadvantage is that individuals outside the system are forced to wait an undetermined period of time before being invited to join a group. We addressed this problem by creating Group

Link, an environment designed to fast-track singles and couples into group life.

Signing People Up

At every monthly Area Fellowship event, the Area Fellowship coordinator asks for a show of hands of those who are not currently in a small group but would like to be. This is a reminder to those who are in small groups to be on the lookout for those who are not. The individuals who raise their hands are asked to sign up for Group Link. The Group Link list is generally located close to the entrance where participants came in.

After the Area Fellowship, the Area Fellowship assimilator and coaches schedule a Group Link event. Invitations are sent to those who put their names on the Group Link list. This event is usually hosted in someone's home. The purpose of the event is to explain North Point's small-group strategy and enlist everyone present into a six-week starter group. Participants are not required to make any commitment to the group beyond the initial six weeks.

Explaining the Strategy

The event itself is centered on a catered meal. When participants show up, they are encouraged to mingle for thirty to forty minutes. Afterward, they are invited to sit down at a table for dinner. Each table or eating area is designed to hold eight to ten people. Participants are allowed to sit wherever they choose.

After dinner the Area Fellowship assimilator explains the Group Link strategy, including the goal for the evening. At the end of the presentation, the assimilator encourages participants to seriously consider beginning a starter group with the people they are seated with. At that time the Area Fellowship coach takes a few minutes to explain what is necessary to become a community group leader. Often people wrongly assume that leading a community group means teaching a Bible study. Once they understand that a community group leader serves as a facilitator, participants are more willing to step forward and assume a leadership role.

Forming Groups

The Group Link event ends with those seated around the tables discussing where and when they could begin meeting as a group. Participants are allowed to switch tables if logistics are a problem. About 80 percent of our starter groups complete the six-week curriculum. More than half of those who complete the six weeks together go on to form a community group.

ED'S TAKE

As I've mentioned, at Fellowship Church the HomeTeams are open, and members are constantly inviting people to attend their next gathering. We make a complete listing of all HomeTeams available to interested persons so they may contact and visit groups near them. We also ask those interested in

HomeTeams to check a box on the worship registration card, contact us through the Web site, or fill out an inquiry card at the booth in our atrium so that we can contact them with more information. HomeTeam builders make these contacts and extend personal invitations to their next meeting. Church staff and the HomeTeam leadership are always recruiting potential builders in hopes of beginning new HomeTeams.

14

the sports ministry

Ed Young

*We have a full-blown athletics ministry
without any permanent recreational facilities.*

The athletics ministry at Fellowship Church began by accident, at least from our perspective (not God's). As far back as 1992, teams from the church began playing in local city recreational leagues. The earliest sports played in those leagues, under the name Fellowship of Las Colinas, were softball, basketball, and football.

Fellowship's official athletics ministry, now called FC Sports, began in 1994, when our singles pastor at the time started using athletics as a way to build relationships among the men and women from our weekend Bible study classes. The ministry quickly caught on and soon became an integral part of what defined our church.

What We Offer

Fellowship Church now offers a year-round athletics calendar that includes the following sports:

- basketball (men's and coed)

- softball (men's and coed)

- flag football (men's and coed)

- volleyball (men's and coed)

- soccer (coed only)

- hockey (mostly men, but women are welcome to play)

Additional leagues are offered seasonally in tennis and golf. In addition, the athletics ministry hosts special events on a limited basis, such as golf tournaments, tennis tournaments, volleyball tournaments, and 5K "fun runs."

Although we have no permanent gymnasium or recreational center (aside from our new youth building for grades six through twelve), we have over three thousand adults involved in the athletics ministry. Through creative thinking and the development of strategic partnerships and relationships, we have developed a full network of off-campus facilities and properties on which we hold 90 percent of our games and leagues. These properties and facilities are generally owned by a city or school district and rented for various fees. The rental fees are factored into each participant's registration costs, thus reducing or eliminating any out-of-pocket expense to the church.

A Natural Inlet to the Church

One of the best things the athletics ministry provides is a comfortable "inlet" to the life of Fellowship Church. People from all walks of life have found a church home at Fellowship simply through the relationships they've built while participating in the various sports we offer.

The captains of all of our sports teams are required to attend a mandatory Team Captains Meeting before all sports seasons begin. At this meeting they are told what the church expects of them as the leader of the team and how we want them to approach this leadership role. They are trained in relationship building and evangelism and challenged to get involved in the lives of their team members. They are encouraged to be aware of and concerned about each player's spiritual growth.

A pre- or post-game devotional and sharing time, generally led by a sports ministry staff member, is built into all games and sports. This time usually includes a personal testimony or word from a team leader or captain. The leader is called upon at random so that the story he or she shares is unrehearsed and original.

Meeting People Where They Are

One of the key things to understand about a ministry like athletics is that you need to reach people where they are, develop relationships with them, and *then* get them involved in the life and ministry of the local church. We have recently renovated an office building that will house a state-of-the-art youth facility with basketball cages, a rock-climbing wall, video and table games, a café, and a meeting room for up to one thousand youth. Much of what will go on in this building will be fun and recreational. But while meeting a basic need for social interaction and entertainment, we will at the same time be introducing youth to the ministry of the church. A year-round sports ministry for adults serves this same purpose.

We shouldn't be ashamed to meet people's recreational and social needs before meeting their spiritual needs. Christ often met a variety of other needs—physical, emotional, social—before he was able to impact people spiritually. At the wedding at Cana, he turned water into wine to make sure the guests had a good time; and in the process, he authenticated his identity and power as the Christ.

Changed Lives through Sports

The sports ministry is a fun and nonthreatening way to get people plugged into the life of the church. Once they've developed relationships with members and regular attenders at Fellowship through recreation, a natural next step is for them to want to know more about Christ. Success stories of people who have come to the church and to a saving knowledge of Christ through athletics are, honestly, too numerous to list. But I want to share one example of how this ministry can truly impact people's lives.

April was a young business executive who played volleyball with her work friends at a local volleyball club. One night, being short of players for her team, she invited several players from the Fellowship Church league (also playing at the same club) to stand in for the missing team members. By the end of the night, April had been invited and convinced to visit Fellowship Church.

The first Sunday she visited, April ended up following her new church friends to the annual Fall Golf Tourney, where she volunteered her time and energy to make this event happen. By the end of her first eight-hour day with Fellowship people, she knew that she had found a new church home. She immediately became a regular and active participant in the church and in the athletics ministry in particular.

Over time April's life began to change and grow as she found spiritual peace and contentment through Christ, along with quality Christian relationships. Now April has stepped into leadership at Fellowship, leading a crew of twelve sports volunteers. She is a living testament to God's ability to change lives through a church athletic program.

ANDY'S TAKE

Call it lack of vision or call it exhaustion, but I cannot imagine hosting an athletic ministry the size of Ed's. We have two softball teams, and two trophies to show for it!

section **3**

leading the church

15

church leadership

Ed Young

We are a staff-led church.

When I say that Fellowship Church is a staff-led church, what do I mean? Simply that the people in the church who are gifted to lead are the ones in leadership positions. We have no elders or deacons; each pastor or director is responsible for the decisions made in his or her department. No one knows the church like the staff, so we believe they should be the ones calling the shots.

We actually have very few staff members for a church with over fifteen thousand in weekend attendance. We could do with a few more, but on the whole, we are doing great with the staff we have. A relatively low number of full-time, paid employees means that we have to make use of laity a lot more. The members have to get more involved in ministry—and that's a win-win situation. Because the people feel a sense of ownership in what we're doing, they develop a loyalty toward the church. And by volunteering to serve the Lord, they develop and mature spiritually.

Staff Accountability

To keep the staff accountable, we have developed a ministry leadership team—a self-perpetuating group of both pastors and laypeople that includes experts in finance, law, and ministry. It is essential for this team to have the same vision for the church that the staff does, so the laypeople in the group are appointed by the staff and approved by a vote of the entire team. This group is a great sounding board and always gives us good input.

Included in the ministry leadership team is the board of trustees. The board works with the financial manager to oversee the day-to-day business side of running the church. They keep us accountable financially, and all outgoing checks must be signed by one of them. This group also has the power to hire and fire the senior pastor.

On the first Wednesday of every March, we present the budget to the membership in a ministry report meeting. We share highlights of the previous year and goals for the upcoming year in a celebration service. We don't open up the floor for questions at that time, but we invite anyone with questions or concerns to call or make an appointment with one of the church management staff.

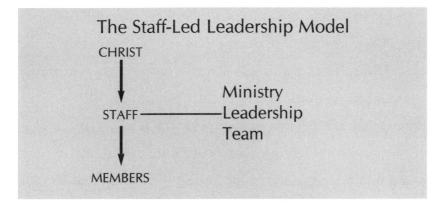

The Staff-Led Leadership Model

The Problem with Committees

Who knows what the youth department needs, the youth pastor or a deacon who has never set foot in the youth department? The youth pastor or a committee of uninformed laypeople who don't understand the goals and needs of that department? In a committee environment, the leaders of different ministries have to argue their case over and over again for each decision they want to make. Naturally, this process takes a lot of time and energy away from the people who could be doing something much more useful elsewhere.

Committees are, for the most part, sedentary bodies. The people on them are not usually active in the day-to-day operations of the church, so it is next to impossible to instill in them the same drive and vision that the staff has. Instead, their attitude becomes "Prove it to me—and let me take my time thinking about it." This is a philosophy destined to wreck the visionary thinking of any church leader.

Most churches are bogged down with a behemoth of boards that allows the church to change course about as quickly as the *Queen Mary.* They can't implement a creative vision that would change the lives of the people in their communities because the bureaucracy and red tape keep them handcuffed.

To me there is nothing more frustrating than sitting in front of a group of people who are completely unconnected to your ministry, with no idea of how it works, trying to convince them to agree with every decision you make. This slow-moving and unresponsive system is the church norm rather than the exception. Is it any wonder that the unchurched often view the church as culturally behind the times and disconnected from their lives?

Why the Staff-Led Model Works

We won't know if something is going to work unless we try it—so we need the ability to give it a shot. We also need to be able to quickly stop trying it when it's obvious that it doesn't work. In a staff-led church, you can jump off a dead horse rather than sitting there atop it while a committee takes its temperature and argues over whether or not it has completely expired. It is crucial to be able to make quick, on-the-dime decisions in our ever changing society. The key element of the staff-led model is that the leaders have the freedom to make those quick decisions.

For example, I recently did a message on discipline from the kids' point of view. It was about the responsibility of children to accept their parents' authority and how God's chain of command works. The arts team came up with a brilliant, hilarious drama—parents on trial for forcing their son to clean his room and do his homework—that led into the 1970s Pink Floyd anthem "Brick in the Wall." They knew that kind of creativity fit in with the vision of the church. They knew that it would exceed people's expectations and impress them. So they went for it. Because the arts team operates on a week-to-week basis, they didn't think of the idea until the Monday before the service. There's no way it could have been approved in time for rehearsal and planning if they'd had to convince a committee that it was a good idea.

This freedom is also essential to our Internet ministry. The World Wide Web is a fast-paced environment, and there is no time to wait when decisions need to be made. Our technology pastor has said that in a committee environment, at least three decisions a day regarding cost, content, and structure would have to be passed by committee members. But if he spent all that time making a case for what he wanted to do, he would never get anything done.

Why It's Unique

Most seminaries don't teach this kind of staff-led model. Instead, models are democratically oriented. Pastors and church leaders taught under this system don't even know that there are other options out there. They have not been equipped with the teaching or the insight to look for a better way, whether they're starting a church or looking for one to pastor.

I don't know who originated the idea that the church, like our society, should be a democracy. The church should be designed as a theocracy: a God-run organization in which he uses gifted leaders to carry out his vision. God did not hesitate to put power into the hands of his Old Testament prophets. He did not ordain a committee of Israelites to follow Elijah, look over his shoulder, and insist that he explain what he was doing at all times so that they could make sure he was in line with God's will. No board of elders was standing off to the side with calculators at Mount Carmel, telling Elijah that he'd better stop at two sets of water rather than three or they would depose him as prophet. Yet somehow, as soon as we start dealing with God's modern-day leaders, we feel that we have to regulate and supervise them to death.

The apostles appointed deacons simply to take care of the day-to-day ministry duties, such as feeding widows and orphans. This allowed the apostles—those gifted in preaching, teaching, and evangelism—to focus on and exercise their gifts. The apostles were certainly accountable to one another (e.g., Paul's rebuke of Peter in Galatians 2), but nowhere were the apostles held accountable to a group of people who didn't understand their unique calling from God.

The Dangers of the Staff-Led Model

Because the staff holds the power in a staff-led church, the danger is that they may abuse that power without a committee overseeing their actions. The safeguard to this is making sure that all pastors are called to their profession by God. They should be people with a clear vision of where God wants them to go and what he wants them to do. Of course, we are all human, and we are all fallible. But I question whether people who are trying, without God's blessing, to lead a church solely in order to glorify themselves are likely to get very far. We've seen examples in the recent past of those who have tried to build ministries on their own power and for their own glory—and great was their fall!

Certainly, I'm not advocating that there be no accountability for the staff or senior pastor. We must all be accountable for our actions, whether to a board of trustees, an elder board, or a congregation. But ultimately, our accountability as pastors is to the Head of the church, Jesus Christ.

ANDY'S TAKE

According to North Point's constitution, we only need congregational approval for five things: selling property, assuming debt, hiring a new senior pastor, changing the constitution, and affiliating the church with a denomination. Like Fellowship Church, we are a staff-led church; but unlike Fellowship, we do have elders—our "guard rails." We have a saying that sums up our church government: We are guided by the staff, guarded by the elders, and gifted by the membership.

The charge of our elders is to monitor my leadership as I monitor the leadership of the staff. The elders function much like a board of directors in a corporation. They approve the budget but do not involve themselves in the day-to-day operations of the church.

16

ministry team representatives

Andy Stanley

What? No deacons?

At North Point Community Church, we do not have deacons. Instead, we have developed a group called Ministry Team Representatives (MTRs). An MTR is an individual chosen by a ministry within the church to represent that group at a quarterly meeting with me and other key staff members. Basically, they represent their area of ministry within a group that represents every area of ministry.

Each group in the church elects one to six MTRs, depending upon the size of the ministry. Currently we have about 90 MTRs representing everything from our production team to our preschool. When I meet with our MTRs, I am meeting with a cross section of all of our leadership. Every interest and perspective is represented. Since their ministry peers have chosen them, they are some of the top leaders within their groups. They groups. They are the influencers—the men and women who make the church work.

Information Exchange

MTR meetings are a time for the open exchange of ideas and information. We spend part of the time reviewing statistical data. We talk about trends, needs, problems, and perceptions. I use MTR meetings as an opportunity to recast the vision of the church. Ministries have an opportunity to give general updates, and staff can present new ministry ideas. Each meeting includes a time for Q & A.

To me, the most beneficial aspect of an MTR meeting is the forum it provides for throwing out new ideas for discussion. This is the ideal environment for floating trial balloons. The opinions expressed by our MTRs reflect the opinions of our church in general. On several occasions our discussions have shown me that my assumptions about what the "church people" thought were dead wrong. Discovering my error directly within the context of an MTR meeting is far safer than discovering it indirectly through the rumor mill.

For example, in 1998 I presented the MTRs with our plan to add additional worship space. To my utter shock, several of the MTRs asked why we needed more space. My initial thought was, *Where have you been for the last three months?* The rest of the staff shared my bewilderment. Fortunately, I held my tongue and listened.

I found out that the MTRs who attend our early service had no idea what was happening in the late service. When they arrived on Sunday morning, there were plenty of parking spaces and several hundred empty seats in our worship center. They didn't know that in the next service the place was bursting at the seams. Their perception of our attendance patterns was not accurate. But perception is everything.

I quickly realized what a mistake it would be to announce our "solution" to the overcrowding problem in our early service. The people would have had the same response as the MTRs in our meeting. And they certainly would not have bought into our plan for creating additional worship space. The remainder of our meeting was spent discussing ways to help our first-service folks understand our overcrowding situation before they had to experience it firsthand.

Financial Clarification

Our MTRs have been extraordinarily helpful to me in determining how to present financial information to the church. In fact, I never present anything to our congregation regarding church finances without presenting it to the MTRs first. As a staff member, I am an insider. I am never fully aware of what the average person in our congregation knows or assumes about our finances. Consequently, when it comes to presenting information, I have a tendency to err on the side of assuming they know more than they do.

Because of my personality, I also have a tendency to err on the side of giving our people more information than they need, want, or can digest. The feedback I receive from our MTRs after a financial presentation is enormously helpful in determining what to present to the congregation. The MTRs are quick to tell me what was confusing, extraneous, or just plain boring. They have a much better idea than I do of the kinds of things people are interested in knowing when it comes to the finances of the church.

Predictable Environments

Every leader needs a predictable, controlled environment in which to think out loud with the influencers of their respective organizations. All too often church leaders go public with a new program or plan for change without checking the organizational temperature first. Since our MTRs represent a microcosm of the entire church, MTR meetings provide the optimal environment for checking that temperature. I never make a decision that will impact the entire church without first presenting it to our MTRs.

When the MTRs have serious reservations about a change, I can expect the same from the congregation. When an idea is a slam-dunk with the MTRs, I can safely assume there will be little disagreement within the congregational ranks as well. The questions raised by our MTRs are the same questions I had better be prepared to answer when I present information to the congregation. Thanks to the honesty and involvement of the MTRs, I am rarely surprised by our church's response to new ideas or program changes.

What? No Deacons?

When I talk to other pastors about our MTRs, they almost always ask, "Why no deacons? The early church appointed deacons. How can you justify a system with no deacons?"

My answer is that the office of deacon is descriptive, not prescriptive. In the Book of Acts, we read that the early church appointed deacons to ease the workload of the apostles. And from what we read in 1 Timothy chapter 3, I think it's safe to assume that the appointment of deacons was common in the early church. At the same time, nowhere is the appointment of deacons commanded or required. Choosing deacons was simply something the early church did to meet a specific need.

The problem with the term "deacon" is that everybody who has grown up in church has a preconceived idea about what that role entails. In the same way that the deacons served to meet the needs of the first century church, I believe our MTRs serve to meet the specific needs of North Point Community Church. For us, MTRs work.

ED'S TAKE

We do not have an organized group of deacons at Fellowship Church. We believe that all servants in the church carry the responsibility of "deacon," although we do not call them by that term.

Like North Point, we are organized into ministry teams. And they are just that: teams doing ministry. I'm convinced that committees waste time, money, and volunteer resources, while accomplishing little over a long period of time. To stay on the cutting edge of ministry and to reach an ever-changing global community, our church has to be able to make the right decisions quickly.

Unlike Andy, I do not meet with lay representatives of our various ministry teams, but rather rely on our staff to be responsible for what occurs within their respective teams. When we have a decision to make, I depend on the staff for their experience and advice. I also have a close circle of trusted friends and experts with whom I may consult; but for the most part, I trust our staff to help determine what's best for the church.

17

hiring the right people

Ed Young

We hire staff from within the church body.

I believe very strongly that the church rises and falls on leadership. You can talk about preaching, drama, events, and children's activities all day and night, but nothing will start going and flowing until you have the right people in leadership positions. For a church to reach its full potential, to become what God has in mind, you must have a strong, hardworking, God-ordained staff in place.

I firmly believe that God places most of our staff members in our churches. It's our mandate to hire these people, to call out their giftedness from the congregation. As Fellowship Church grows, we have to add staff positions quite frequently. Of course, choosing the right person for the job is essential. And almost always, we find that right person from within our own membership.

When we realize that a certain job is going to require a staff position, we look at who is already taking care of the task. Is a layperson carrying the full weight of the work on his or her shoulders, along with a full-time job? Is a staff member responsible, while getting plenty of help from volunteers? Chances are there are already people stepping up who are ready to take it on full time.

Why Hire Members?

We rarely hire people from outside the church because there are so many benefits to hiring people we already know. We know they have given financially and have been active in the church. We know they support the church vision and work well in our unique environment. We've observed their talents and gifts and know that they are capable. We know they're loyal; they're already emotionally committed to the church, and they're not planning on going anywhere. Most importantly, we know they have a heart for God. Furthermore, laypeople who are hired from within the church generally aren't expecting to be offered a job; they know that it's a God thing from the beginning, and they continue to look to him for inspiration.

Hire for the Heart, Not Just the Head

You may be wondering how we manage to find enough formally trained, seminary-schooled pastors milling around among the laity to staff our church. The answer is very simple:

We don't. We don't think, in our style of church, that people who are formally trained are the only ones qualified to lead. We don't think that seminary is necessary for all positions—Pastor of Technology, for example—and we don't have a problem with hiring women for key staff positions. Just because someone knows *Koine* Greek doesn't mean he or she will be a skilled leader, in touch with the church's vision, and motivated to push forward.

It is more important for you to hire someone with the right heart than someone with all the right head knowledge. I'm not saying you should divorce your leaders from their brains. You still have to have intelligent people and strategic thinkers on board. But I'm saying that if you are wavering between the candidate with the right head and the candidate with the right heart, go with the heart.

Let's say candidate number one, Ben, is on fire for the Lord. He has more drive, motivation, and energy than anyone you've ever met. But he's never been to seminary, and he has little technical knowledge of the Bible. Candidate number two, Jerry, looks like the perfect staff member. He graduated magna cum laude from one of the most prestigious seminaries in the country. He's already written three books, two of which made the bestseller list. He would be a fabulous asset to your leadership team. You don't see the same drive in him that you see in Ben, the same all-out fire for God, but you're sure that his credentials will make up for that.

Wrong. It's the other way around. Ben's heart will more than make up for what he lacks in the head. But Jerry's head can never fill in for what he lacks in the heart. Think of it this way: Ben can learn the head knowledge he should have for his position. But no class will teach Jerry how to have a true heart for God. This is the best reason for hiring people from within the membership: Because you know them, you know if they have the right heart.

What Is the Right Heart?

There are usually three characteristics that tip you off to the people who have the right heart: They are *teachable*, they are *flexible*, and they are *loyal*. I want to be teachable as a pastor, and I want our staff to be teachable. If a person isn't teachable, he or she won't make it on our church staff. Staff members have to be willing to put the best interests of the church over their own best interests.

People with the right heart are also flexible. At Fellowship Church, we change a lot. From week to week, from month to month, from year to year, we change. We've gone from a church of 150 to a church of 15,000. That in itself has brought about many changes. When we bring on new staff members, we let them know that they might not be in that position a year from now, five years from now, ten years from now. As the church grows and expands and changes, so will the staff positions we need. We may change people around. We may take one person's job, split it in two, and hire someone else to take up the slack. That means flexibility is critical.

Finally, people with the right heart are loyal. In fact, loyalty is the most important of the three characteristics. We want to hire people who are loyal to the vision of Fellowship Church and loyal to each other. The staff must function in an atmosphere of trust, knowing that each person will take care of the other and stick up for the other. I can't think of anything that will destroy the morale of a staff and the vision of a church faster than backbiting or backstabbing.

What You Need to Do It Right

Obviously, to hire from within the membership, church leaders must have discernment. Because we have a staff-led model of government, anyone brought on as staff is going to have a lot of responsibility. If the music directors are the only people responsible for choosing the music, then we have to be able to trust them not to use an inappropriate song. We have to make sure they truly want to serve and not just fulfill their own personal agenda.

How do we have discernment? At Fellowship, the people in leadership positions spend a lot of time building relationships with their volunteers. Each of our ministries holds weekly Bible studies and monthly vision meetings to keep on track.

Especially in the music and drama departments, where people are more likely to get star-struck because they're on stage, the leaders emphasize that they're involved in ministry, not a show. When you spend time with the people working with you, it is a lot easier to figure out where their hearts are.

Interview, Interview, Interview

Does all this emphasis on knowing our volunteers, knowing who we're hiring, mean that we don't interview them? Absolutely not. It is so important to have the right staff that we don't want to take a chance on someone—even someone we know—without running their candidacy by everyone we can lay our hands on.

When we're looking at prospective staff members, we have them sit down with every member of our management team. We talk to them and ask them questions to see if they are teachable, flexible, and loyal. We also do background checks and psychological profiles. We truly want to leave no stone unturned.

Also, we never hire someone without talking to his or her spouse. We want to see how the prospective staff member and his or her mate interact. So along with interviewing the couple, we'll take them out to do something socially—dinner or golf or whatever. We want to see how they connect with one another. That tells us a great deal about how the person will relate with others and fit into our staff.

Yeah, Right!

Still not convinced that hiring from within can work? Let me tell you a story. When the pastoral search team of Fellowship Church brought me to Dallas to interview me for this job, they began to ask me questions about what kind of staff I might need. About five of them were looking at me. I looked back and said, "Well, you're going to be my staff. Obviously, we can't pay you right now. But I'm going to ask you to commit to being at the church whenever possible and not miss a weekend for the next year." And they did. Now three of those five people are full-time staff members.

One of those three is Preston Mitchell. Preston had a great job at a large corporation. Whenever he wasn't at work, he was at the church. When I would go out to visit people who had come to the church, he would go with me. He opened up his home to us for Bible studies and for socializing. Preston and his wife were pivotal to the success of Fellowship Church in those days.

Several years ago I was thinking about our staffing needs and wondering who we were going to bring in for a certain position. At the same time, Preston was feeling called to leave his job of fifteen years and go into the ministry. It clicked. We interviewed him—yes, even this founding member of the church—and brought him on board. His wife and children had no idea that one day he would be a full-fledged ordained pastor. He's now on our management team as pastor of spiritual development. What a great success story!

ANDY'S TAKE

I am in total agreement with Ed when it comes to who and how you hire. More than 90 percent of our full- and part-time staff began as volunteers. People often ask me, "Where do you find such quality people?" The answer is simple: Quality attracts quality. Quality churches attract quality people. And among those quality people, you will find quality staff.

Our interview process is very thorough—some would say brutal. Interviewees consistently remark that our process is the most comprehensive they have ever experienced. We require potential staff members to take three tests and interview with at least four staff members outside the department that is hiring them. My assistant interviews every candidate.

We enjoy very little staff turnover. To date, six people have transitioned off of our staff. All of them still attend our church.

18

storytelling

Andy Stanley

*We share ministry stories during staff meetings
for inspiration and instruction.*

One of the biggest challenges for leaders is keeping the mission and values of the organization in front of their leadership. These days most churches have a mission statement hanging on the wall somewhere. Most have a list of values printed in an employee handbook. But how do you keep that kind of information in front of your key leaders? More importantly, how do you know that they have actually bought into the mission and values of your ministry?

One thing that we have found to be extraordinarily effective at North Point Community Church is to begin leadership meetings by opening up the floor for storytelling. Every Monday morning at our staff meeting, I open our time together with this question: What happened yesterday (Sunday) or last week in your area of ministry that made you feel as if you had made progress leading people into a growing relationship with Christ? Then I sit back and listen.

This is probably the most encouraging thirty minutes of my week. About one-third of those in attendance will share a personal story of something that happened in their ministry that is directly related to the mission of our church.

Teachable Moments

As I listen, I look for opportunities to interject the relationship between what is being shared and our core values. These teachable moments provide me with some of the best opportunities I have for leadership training with our staff.

Stories give life to mission statements and values. It is one thing for me to encourage our staff to develop relationships with unbelievers. But nothing I can say will ever be as impacting as, for example, our production director talking about what it was like to take a Sunday off so she could attend worship with an unbelieving friend with whom she has been building a relationship for several months.

Stories bring life to what, over time, can become lifeless organizational jargon. An experience overlays our well-crafted statements with emotion and, at times, passion. A personal illustration within this context clarifies and more clearly defines our mission in the minds of those listening. This approach to rehearsing the mission and values of an organization is far more memorable than reviewing a list of terms and definitions.

Celebrating Success

Storytelling also provides an opportunity for our staff to celebrate successes cross-departmentally. A growing organization can easily become a fragmented organization. Before long everybody is spinning in their own departmental orbit, unaware of what is happening down the hall. Providing our staff with an opportunity to share their success stories allows our leaders to temporarily enter the world of their coworkers. Everybody leaves with an enhanced understanding of, and greater appreciation for, what the other ministries are doing.

Team building hinges on individuals experiencing the synergy that results from working strategically with others. Just about every week, someone will share a story of how an individual in another ministry area supported what he or she was doing. By bragging across departmental lines, staff members underscore their appreciation for and dependency upon other areas of our ministry. These are powerful and often tearful moments.

In addition to looking for teachable moments, I look for opportunities to spotlight success stories I have seen or heard about. Anytime I receive an encouraging letter that mentions our staff or an individual staff member, I always make a point to read it to the whole group on Monday morning.

Evaluation

A secondary benefit to beginning our staff meetings with storytelling is that it forces everyone in attendance to do some personal evaluation. When I ask the group to share what they experienced during the previous seven days that serves as evidence that they have been successful in accomplishing the mission of the church, everybody begins evaluating. Specifically, they hold up the events of the previous week against the backdrop of what we have defined as success for our organization.

I can see it in the expressions on their faces. They are thinking back. They are evaluating. That one question in this highly relational environment creates an optimal opportunity for personal and professional evaluation. After all, when two of your peers update the group on the progress they've made with unbelieving friends, and you don't have any unbelieving friends, that is going to cause you some healthy discomfort. When the person on your right celebrates a breakthrough he or she experienced in a small group, and you still haven't joined a group, you are going to feel some tension. We close our sharing time by breaking up into groups of four and five and praying together.

By modeling the tool of storytelling with our staff, it has become intuitive for them to begin their departmental leadership meetings the same way. As a result, our mission and values are reinforced at every level.

ED'S TAKE

I agree wholeheartedly with this practice. At Fellowship Church, we are very intentional about storytelling in our staff meetings. I make sure the staff hears about life-change stories because these stories can energize and motivate them in an incredible way.

I love to tell stories about everyday life. In staff meetings, I tell stories about the stuff that happens in my life, and we share stories about both the heart-wrenching and crazy things that happen to all of us in ministry. This creates a good environment for me to point out some of the mistakes we have made, vision cast, or just get to know the staff on a more personal basis. Our staff meetings include spiritual reflection and gales of laughter. We have fun.

I also like to tell stories about Fellowship Church's past. Reminiscing about some of the things we've done in the past helps our new staff members relate to the history of our church. These stories give them a glimpse back in time and help them understand why we are the church we are today.

We also tell life-change stories during weekend services. In fact, we've done an entire message series called "FC: True Fellowship Stories," using videotaped true stories of people whose lives have been radically changed through the ministry of our church. Not only do these stories impact people in very significant ways, but they also show that Fellowship is still reaching people. These accounts are as much about vision casting as life change, because we believe a church should always be asking the question, "Is it still working?" The stories communicate a resounding "Yes!"

getting the message across

19

sermon planning

Ed Young

*We make the message the first priority of the service—
and of the pastor.*

A good restaurant has a balanced menu, with a wide variety of appetizers, salads, entrees, and desserts. Similarly, at Fellowship Church we try to provide a balanced spiritual menu of sermons covering a wide range of practical themes: family, relationships, character, marriage, core values, and the like, along with relevant concentrations on biblical books or figures. The community has a need for practical Bible knowledge that is applicable to daily life, and we try to meet that need in timely and culturally relevant ways.

For example, in 1999 I did a series called Know Fear: Facing Life's Phobias, which addressed all the anxiety surrounding Y2K. Each week I focused on a different fear that we all face: the fear of the future, the fear of death, the fear of commitment, the fear of failure, and the fear of loneliness. In the last message of the series, I talked about some common misconceptions about the fear of God, and then explained the biblical idea of fearing God. The main idea was that a proper fear of God— reverence for and trust in God—alleviates the other fears and phobias we face in life. Everyone deals with fear, and placing this series within the context of the Y2K crisis helped bring the truth of the Bible, literally, into the 21st century.

Each message series usually lasts four to six weeks, although I have gone for as long as fourteen weeks (with X-Trials, a series on the Book of James) and as short as two (with a quick series called Got Stress?). Occasionally it happens that there is a short, one- or two-week break between specifically planned series. I might use that space for a unique evangelistic appeal—like a message I did called "Lifelines," where I handed out Lifesavers candy as a reminder to reach out to people who are lost. A short space also works well for a vision-casting message.

In a typical year, I try to cover many different topics in a balanced way. For example, in 1996 I did series on:

- The state of the church
- Basic life principles
- The family
- Spiritual maturity
- An expositional study (of Psalm 23 or Galatians 5, for example)
- Vision

- Relationships (dating and/or marriage)

- Seasonal themes (at Christmas, Easter, or Thanksgiving)

Other years have been similarly balanced.

Research and Message Preparation

A crucial aspect of sermon planning is the actual research and preparation of the weekend message. But for the busy pastor with a myriad of assignments and appointments, this task can be overwhelming. Family, personal time, community events, church administration—they all clamor for attention.

Spending twenty-five to thirty hours a week on sermon preparation seems impossible for most pastors. Yet most good communicators will tell you that it takes at least that much time each week to adequately prepare for the weekend message. How can you get it all done and still have time to fulfill your primary calling as a preacher of God's Word?

Research, I've found, must be a daily undertaking. With or without an assistant, you must constantly be learning, observing, and categorizing information for later use. The more organized you are, the better off you'll be as you prepare your sermons each week. It helps to delegate different aspects of research—maybe looking up a statistic that would support a particular point—to other staff members. If you involve your staff in long-range sermon planning, they will know the kinds of information that will help you in the near future. Select staff members can look ahead at the sermon schedule and help you glean relevant information from commentaries and other resources. They can also keep you up-to-date on the news of the day by scanning the daily newspaper, weekly news magazines, and Christian periodicals.

If you have a hard time studying at the office, by all means go somewhere else to do it. I do the lion's share of my studying at Starbucks, with my Bible and legal pad in hand. I've found that changing environments can serve to foster more creative ideas. But whatever you have to do and wherever you have to go to adequately prepare your messages, get it done. Set your boundaries and stick to them, because no one else can do it for you. Don't let the tyranny of the urgent drag you away from the important task of understanding and communicating God's truth to those who desperately need it.

The Primacy of the Pulpit

You must continually reaffirm your primary calling as a preacher of God's Word and give it priority. And the leaders of your church must give it the same priority. They are going to have to be involved in protecting your schedule. This may mean hiring additional staff members to take on other aspects of the ministry that are demanding inordinate amounts of your time.

At Fellowship Church, we recognize that the weekend message has the potential to reach more people for Christ than any other ministry of the church. Thousands of people hear the message each weekend, with hundreds visiting the church for the first time. That means my first priority must be to communicate God's unchanging truth in relevant and life-changing ways.

Other tasks can be done by others—and often much better. For example, I recognize that my gifts do not lie in the area of counseling. I admit that openly: I am not a good counselor. God has called me to be a preacher, a communicator of his Word. At Fellowship, we have hired other pastors to do the job of individual and family counseling. When people want to see me for counseling, I unhesitatingly refer them to one of the other pastors. If you're in a small church and don't have other staff available, consider partnering with an outside counselor or counselors to whom you can refer people.

This is just one area that can take a great deal of a pastor's time. What are the areas that are taking you away from your primary ministry? Once you've identified them, get together with your leaders and figure out a way to restore the primacy of the pulpit in your church. There's no greater calling in the world. Give it the priority it deserves.

ANDY'S TAKE

Like Ed, I find that sermon preparation takes the lion's share of my time. I set aside every Wednesday and Thursday to study. Unlike Ed, I prefer to study in isolation. I have two preferred study environments: at the church and by the lake. Most of the time I prepare at the church in a small, thirteen-by-thirteen-foot room creatively referred to as my "study." It is accessed through my office and contains a desk, bookshelf, planning board, and filing cabinets. When I'm in the study, the staff knows I am off limits.

Occasionally I make the forty-five minute drive to a church member's lake house and spend the day studying on the back porch. If I feel the need to be completely inaccessible, I head to the lake. These days are like personal retreats. I keep a briefcase full of study helps in the trunk of my car just in case I make a last-minute decision to head out of town for the day.

In addition to studying on Wednesday and Thursday, I spend three or four hours on Saturday night reviewing and memorizing my message. Since I plan my sermons well in advance, that Saturday night review is often the first time I have looked at that particular outline in two or three weeks. Consequently, I generally make extensive last-minute changes. This is one of the negatives of working so far ahead. Over time, however, I have grown to appreciate the value of coming back to a message with fresh eyes. My Saturday-night editing sessions generally result in a tighter, more focused outline.

preaching calendar

Andy Stanley

*We are intentional and deliberate
in the timing and topics of our sermon series.*

How often do you find yourself asking the daunting question, "What should our next series of sermons address?"? At North Point Community Church, our planning team faced that question every four to eight weeks. Now we've developed a preaching calendar that has given us a built-in system for determining our series. We've discovered that categorizing our series according to the time of year greatly facilitates the process of determining series topics. We have identified nine categories that we feel are critical to a balanced preaching calendar.

Series by the Season

Spring

We begin our preaching calendar in the spring. Spring has two categories. The first, The Big Hook, highlights Easter. Easter usually brings our once-a-year visitors, and we feel like we need to do something that will draw them back the following Sunday.

The second category is Relationships. With Mother's Day beginning and Father's Day ending this time frame, we use this category to promote the importance of godly relationships between family members and others.

Summer

After Father's Day we begin summer with a category called Creatively Linked Random Topics. This category consists of stand-alone messages that are connected by a theme. We have found this type of series to be appropriate in light of our summer attendance pattern.

Fall

In the fall we focus on personal growth, since it's the beginning of the school year, and most people are ready to begin learning again. The first category, Regrouping, starts after Labor Day. This category concentrates on practical spiritual growth. The second category, Spiritual Life, addresses inner spiritual growth and focuses on the transforming power of the Christian journey.

Winter

We fill our winter slate with four categories. The first, Seasonal, begins at Thanksgiving and lasts until Christmas. The purpose of this series is to prepare our church for the celebration of Christ's birth. We begin the new year with a two- to three-week series focused on the mission and vision of our church. We refer to this as our Strategic Series.

In February and March, we wrap a series around a book of the Bible. We refer to this as our Bible Book Series. This is the longest series we do—usually eight to ten weeks. Depending upon the length of the book, this is either a verse-by-verse study or a survey of key passages.

Pre-Easter is the final category of the winter season. Generally, this is a straight-ahead evangelistic series. There are two reasons we choose to focus on evangelism just before Easter. First, it reminds our people of the opportunity they have to invite friends to our Easter services. Second, we know that there are many nonbelievers who have been attending since the previous Easter. We want to make sure they have had an opportunity to formally accept Christ as Savior before we launch into a new season.

Series Overview

The list below reflects our preaching calendar with suggested time frames and topics. While we may not adhere strictly to the time frame outlined, we are faithful to the categories.

1. *The Big Hook*
- Spring: Four to six weeks beginning with Easter
- Topics: adversity, heaven and hell, decision making, stress

2. *Relationships*
- Spring: Six weeks, Mother's Day to Father's Day
- Topics: family, friendship, love, dating, marriage, children

3. *Creatively Linked Random Topics*
- Summer: Two five-week sessions
- Topics: Bible characters, moral issues, doctrines, random questions

4. *Regrouping*
- Fall: Six weeks beginning Labor Day
- Topics: stewardship, evangelism, devotional life

5. *Spiritual Life*
- Late fall: Six weeks
- Topics: faith, prayer, intimacy with God, worship

6. *Seasonal*
- Winter: Three to four weeks, Thanksgiving to Christmas
- Topics: God's love for us, grace, different perspectives on the birth of Jesus

7. *Strategic Series*
- Early winter: Two weeks beginning with the New Year
- Topics: values, vision, mission, small group strategy

8. *Bible Book Series*
- Winter: Ten weeks
- Topics: random books of the Bible

9. *Pre-Easter*

- Late winter: Four to six weeks
- Topics: miracles, eternal security, salvation, forgiveness, the Second Coming

Within each category each year, four or five of the topics will be new and four or five of the topics will be renewed from previous years. By repeating a topic, we can make a good series better. Our goal is to repeat selected series every three to five years.

ED'S TAKE

I typically plan my preaching schedule around our church attendance patterns. From day one I have asked our staff to count every person who comes to our worship services. We counted when we had 150 people, and we count now that we have more than 15,000.

Why is counting so important? We don't count people so that we can pat ourselves on the back about our growth. We count people so that we can build data on church attendance. I am always amazed at how our data matches from one year to the next. The numbers change, but the percentages throughout each year stay the same. There is a definite ebb and flow to the life of Fellowship Church.

As a pastor, you need to know the attendance patterns of your church. The data will help prepare you for expected growth, message series, big events, and (last but not least) your vacation time. You have got to strategically plan time away, especially on those weekends that you know are low attendance times. It's important to recharge your batteries. My father, even in the early days of his ministry at Second Baptist Houston, always took off the month of June.

Month-by-Month Strategy

The ebb and flow of Fellowship Church goes something like this:

January and February

I miss the weekend after New Year's Day because most of our regular attendees are still on vacation. Besides, I'm still recovering from speaking seven times on Christmas Eve weekend.

I begin a new series the second weekend of January. This is one of the three most important series of the year (along with Easter and the start of school in the fall). The weeks leading up to Spring Break are great growth times for our church.

March

In the Dallas/Fort Worth area, three weekends are affected by Spring Break. I usually take one or two weekends off during that span. This is a great time to focus on singles because they are still around the church while all the families are off on vacation. One year I did a series on dating that attracted large numbers of singles during the month of March. Our singles ministry uses that time to promote their activities.

We also begin planning a community-wide direct-mail campaign to send out to promote the Easter weekend, targeting hundreds of thousands of homes within a ten-mile radius of the church. We've found this is an opportune time to plan an expansion of our worship bulletin to showcase all the ministries of our church on Easter weekend. But the planning and preparation has to start early.

April

For many years I have started a new series on Easter weekend. I try to choose a series that will have the most impact on unchurched people because of the large numbers of seasonal churchgoers (those who come just at Easter and Christmas). For example, I may begin a series on marriage or parenting, with a hook to get people back the next weekend. Of course, I always work in the gospel message of the death, burial, and resurrection of Jesus. The series I start on Easter will usually go through Mother's Day.

In terms of format, we try to do our Easter service the same way we do every weekend service. We want people to experience what happens at Fellowship Church on nonevent weekends.

May

After Mother's Day attendance begins to flatten a little. People in Dallas/Fort Worth are enjoying the beautiful spring weather, and school is coming to a close. I do a short series between Mother's Day and Memorial Day weekend. I take off Memorial Day weekend because it is one of the lowest-attended weekends of the year.

June

June is a time when I plan special, one-time weekend events. Because I am gone most of the month attending our student camps and retreats, I don't want to worry about studying for a series. During this time we may have a baptismal celebration or a weekend highlighting the life-change stories of people in the congregation. We may plan a student weekend to highlight our camps.

July

I rarely speak during this month. I take July off and use the time as a study break and family vacation time. I also meet with our creative team and plan the topics for the next twelve months. During this month off, our worship services are planned around a series, but other members of my staff do the speaking. We are blessed at Fellowship to have several talented staff members who can preach and teach.

It is vital for you to develop people to replace you so that you can take time off. I recommend that you develop speaking talent internally rather than inviting guest speakers from other churches to fill the pulpit. The church needs to get used to the idea that the senior pastor cannot speak every weekend and that other staff members are ready and capable of taking up the charge. Part of the pastor's leadership role is to train up other staff who can teach the body. Your vacation times are excellent opportunities for the people to benefit from and learn to trust other key leaders.

Oftentimes, if I am in town, I will show up at church and do the welcome or the announcements. This communicates to the congregation that I'm there but I'm not speaking. I also shoot video introductions of the other speakers ahead of time for the weekends I am gone. That is an effective way for people who are visiting to know who I am even when I am out of town.

August

August is a huge growth time for us—especially the three weekends between the start of school and Labor Day weekend. For this reason, the series I begin the second weekend of August is one of the most important of the year. We also do another massive direct-mail campaign to promote and kick off the fall. I don't normally miss Labor Day weekend, primarily because I've already missed several weeks during the summer.

September through November

I do one or two series during the fall. Attendance flattens a little after Labor Day weekend. I always miss Thanksgiving weekend because attendance is low for us.

December

I plan a short series (three weeks or so) leading up to Christmas Eve. On Christmas Eve, which is second only to Easter in attendance, we have multiple worship services. This is a community event that we promote heavily, because people love to come to church on Christmas Eve. I do not preach the last weekend of December or the first weekend of January because of the holidays. During the time I am off, I begin planning for the important start of the New Year, which for us starts the second weekend in January.

21

creativity

Ed Young

*We creatively adapt the service and the worship center
to enhance a creative message.*

During the ten years of Fellowship Church's life, we have learned that creativity is pivotal to building an exciting church that will make a difference in people's lives. Creativity brings people in the front door, and creativity keeps people from going out the back door. It doesn't matter the size of the church, its makeup, its budget, or the demographics: Creativity can be applied in all situations.

Creativity is closely linked to change. At Fellowship we keep all aspects of the service in a constant state of flux from week to week. Sometimes the band is close to the audience; sometimes it's farther back. We change the color of the backdrop, the order of the service, and the style of the music. We completely rework the bulletin for each series, changing its size, shape, and color scheme. Sometimes I speak from a Plexiglas lectern; sometimes I use a stool. I have led live sheep on stage, driven a car across the platform, ridden a camel up to our church doors, and demonstrated with a fly rod in the middle of a message. All these things contribute to total sensory communication—to reaching our audience through every avenue possible.

Theology of Creativity

Did we just dream up this kind of creative communication from thin air? No. Creativity is biblical. After all, it's the fifth word in the Bible: "In the beginning, God created." God created the entire universe, from the infinite complexity of a single cell to the vast cosmos of far-off galaxies—and Ephesians 5:1 commands us to imitate him. God is creative, and he has created us in his image as creative beings. We can't tell him, "Look, I just don't have a creative bone in my body." That kind of weak excuse makes a mockery of what God has done in creating us.

I laugh when the media suddenly highlights a church that is creative. It's such a big deal: "Wow, look at what that church is doing! They're being creative! I can't believe it! I've never seen anything like it!" Creativity should be the norm. People should expect churches to be creative—and be surprised when they're boring. The churches that are dull should stick out rather than the ones that are creative.

The problem is that somewhere along life's journey, most of us get a creative cramp. We trade in dreaming for dogma, the artistic for the analytical. We trade in using our imaginations for memorization. We float around in the shallows of sameness rather than riding on the crest of creativity. How can we reach our full potential? How can we use creativity to glorify God in the way he wants us to when the world tends to squeeze it out of us?

I've been journaling my prayers since I was eighteen years old. From time to time I like to flip back through the journals to see if there are any trends, anything in particular I should be focusing on. Several years ago, as I was thumbing through a prayer journal, I noticed that at least once a week I was praying for creativity—asking God to stretch me, to open up new areas to me, to help me think in unique, creative ways. And he has answered! I believe that if you pray that way, God will unleash your unique creativity too.

Elements of Creativity

There are two elements to the practice of creativity: change and visuals. People get bored with seeing and hearing the same old thing week after week. When they know what's coming, they tune it out; the higher the predictability, the lower the communication. Constant change gives a look of freshness and keeps people interested.

The best compliment you can hear about your church is, "I never know what they're going to do next!"

Visuals are invaluable in this respect. Most people will remember something they've heard for a longer period of time if they see it demonstrated visually. Jesus recognized this—that's why he spoke from hillsides, beaches, and boat bows; it's why he picked up a pebble, pointed to a sower, drew in the sand, and put a child in his lap.

For a series for singles called The Ulti-Mate, I came up with the idea of comparing "that special someone" to a luxury car. Looking in the trunk was a parallel for finding out the other person's emotional baggage; looking behind the wheel symbolized finding out who's driving the relationship (Jesus, or someone else?); and taking the car off-road was a word picture for misusing God's gift of sexuality. To demonstrate these ideas, I wanted to drive a car across the stage—a Mercedes 500SL to be exact. A man who's been visiting our church for some time owns a car dealership, and he was able to set us up with one of these fantastic vehicles for the two weekends I needed it.

Another time I did a message called "Lifelines," which discussed how each of us might be the only eternal lifeline in an unbeliever's life. Not only did we put a boat up on stage and show a vignette from the television show *Rescue 911* just before the message, we set bags of individually wrapped Lifesaver candies at the end of each row and had the audience pass them out during the service. I told the people to think of one person in their lives that they knew needed Christ—someone who was drowning—and to pray for them and invite them to church. When the person accepted Christ, they could eat the Lifesaver.

Building in Creativity Time

How do we come up with these ideas? Two or three times a year, I have a massive meeting with our arts team—two music directors and a drama director. We plan out the next few series, decide what topics we want to cover, and determine how many weeks each one will be. Once we have that general outline to work from, we come up with most of our creative ideas during brainstorming sessions in our weekly staff meetings.

The staff at Fellowship Church is fantastic. We meet regularly and talk often. Most of our planning is done on a week-to-week basis, although a video segment may be shot a month or so in advance. Everyone contributes and has something creative and valuable to add. Because it's such an open environment, no one is afraid to take a risk or say that an idea won't work. Everything that eventually gets onstage is going to fall short of what we discuss in these brainstorming sessions anyway, so we shoot for the stars. We can pull crazy, unfeasible ideas back down to the level of reality later. Creativity breeds creativity.

I can't emphasize enough how important it is that nothing be left off the table. One of our brainstorming sessions generated an idea for a series called Listen to the Music. We started out the service with a secular song on a certain theme and included a little Motown revue—with backup singers and the works. After the message we ended with a song with Christian lyrics focusing on the same theme. The idea had seemed farfetched at the time, but the service turned out to be quite effective.

It's essential to communicate this level of drive and creativity to your staff. The staff at Fellowship knows that I expect them to be creative, to go beyond what we usually do, to keep everything changing. I want them to take risks, even though that means they will fail sometimes.

From there, it's just a matter of implementing the ideas—which is no easy task. For the Mercedes visual, we had to rehearse the message multiple times, practicing the drive on and off the stage and figuring out where I would stand at different points in the service. It took six people backstage to set up the car and take care of it once I drove it off.

On the Same Page

The creativity quotient plays a huge part in how far in advance we need to plan. Obviously, more elaborate visuals, videos, or dramas require more advanced planning. And even though we have full-time staff who oversee the stage management, lighting, props, and whatever else is needed to make the service happen, we know that we can overload them with work if our creativity gets out of control. We do try to stagger the more elaborate services so that we don't drain our staff's resources on a weekly basis. A poorly planned and executed service doesn't bring glory to God and can turn people away from the message.

We've found that our effectiveness is a matter of communication and having everyone on the same page. If I'm planning to discuss adoption into the family of God, for example, the arts team needs to know whether I'm going to focus on the salvation message or talk about who we are in Christ. They need to know if the service is going to be hard-hitting or lighter in tone. This knowledge then guides their decisions about appropriate music, drama, and visuals.

Typically they start by asking one simple question: "What haven't we done in a while?" If we've used videos in the previous two services, they will try to avoid them for the upcoming weekend. If we haven't done a drama in a month, then they're likely to do one. They pick out all the music, trying to keep the atmosphere fresh. They might bring in a different, creative instrument like a cello or bagpipes. They might use a dancer. If it's for the glory of God, we say, go for it!

Our worship center was specifically designed with this kind of creativity in mind. The stage is huge and provides great flexibility. Two immense screens are on either side. We have the ability to do a lot with lighting, sound, and video. The facility is functional, not opulent, and everything focuses inward toward what's happening onstage. We have a balcony we can block off and a curtain below it so that the auditorium can seat eighteen hundred, twenty-eight hundred, or forty-one hundred people, letting us create a packed feeling even for smaller events.

Putting Things in Order

The order of the service is an important component of creative planning. A worship service is a series of moments, and the people planning it need to understand how that works. A funny, upbeat, and lighthearted drama creates a very different kind of moment than a moving song, and it's poor planning to pile the two on top of each other.

One weekend we did a very emotional and touching service focusing on the moving testimony of a family at the church. We specifically arranged to take the offering before the message began, since we didn't want to ruin the moment at the end of the service by passing the plates. We also made that weekend's service a "mystery topic"—we didn't publicize it the week before so that the story could have its full effect.

The key is for everything to work together. No element should be able to stand on its own. The drama, music, singing, visuals, lighting, props, and message should work together to create one cohesive, effective service.

In the process, it's important to be flexible. If something is not working—if the drama doesn't make the point it is meant to, or a complex visual onstage just isn't working out—you have to be able to change. We meet after the Saturday night service to discuss how it went, and it's not unusual for us to change the order of the service for the next morning. We may cut a song or drama or add a video we hadn't planned on using. We may change where a band member stands or add a guitar solo. We ask, "Did we make the moment?" And if we didn't, we try something else on Sunday.

This kind of flexibility only works, however, if everyone is willing to be objective despite their personal, vested interests in their portion of the service. What is important is that the temple gets built. It doesn't matter who builds it.

The Centrality of Scripture

This brings us to an important reason for careful planning: ensuring that the message of the Bible is the central focus of the weekend services. Visuals can be illuminating. Videos can move and inspire. Lights and props and drama can keep people interested. But too much of a good thing can quickly distract from the very reason people need to be there, which is to apply the Word of God to their lives. While creativity should be planned into each sermon series, people can grow tired of what I call "uncontrolled creative cramming." When the creative aspects of the service overpower the message, then you have not planned well.

Excessive creative cramming results in a drowned audience. You've got to know when enough is enough and even when to cut back. Every so often—usually after a particularly multisensory weekend—we go back and do a simplistic service. We've found that a basic meat-and-potatoes message makes the more creative services stand out. Without balance you can lose perspective and fall into creative overload. There is simply too much going on. The service is too busy. Too many elements, even if they are all good, creative ideas, just lead to a sensory storm. If it doesn't serve to underscore the theme, then it's unnecessary. If you have to explain it too much, then it's a bad visual.

Creative Titles

In my opinion titles are one of the church's most overlooked opportunities. At Fellowship, our message titles, series titles, and program titles are all designed to gain the immediate interest of the reader and creatively communicate an idea. This isn't for the benefit of our members; it's to draw the unchurched in. For example, I did a series called FC: True Fellowship Stories that played off the popular *E: True Hollywood Story* cable television show. In another series, I did a message on the camel going through the eye of a needle and called it "Camel Filter." The title is the first impression we make and the first chance we get to attract someone to our church.

A Difficult Task

I'm not saying that thinking creatively is easy. If it were simple, everyone would do it. In reality, being creative is the most draining thing we do at Fellowship; it's a lot of trouble and takes a lot of time, energy, and money. The Bible is a complex book, and our job is to make it easy to understand. That's difficult.

As a church, we are going to fail. As leaders, we are going to fail. We are human and we are fallible, and there's just no way around it. The question is, how are we going to fail? I am committed to fail going forward. As John Maxwell says in his book *Fail Forward*, fail forward, not backward! Fail because you took a risk on a creative idea, not because you refused to take any action at all.

I'm not just talking about being a contemporary church. Many contemporary churches are stuck in a rut, doing the same old thing. It doesn't matter that the same old thing is something contemporary; when people hear the same thing over and over in the same way, they stop listening. Failure is doing the same thing the same way and expecting unique results. At Fellowship we are committed to communicating timeless truths in creative ways, and so far the results have been unique!

We are creatures of habit. But when the psalmist says, "Sing to the LORD a new song" (Psalm 96:1), he is urging us out of our comfort zones and toward a commitment to innovative and creative change to the glory of God. Biblical change produces growth. And when real spiritual growth begins to occur within a congregation, it is infectious. People you could never have dreamed of reaching will be drawn to the church, and lives will be changed.

ANDY'S TAKE

We also put a lot of time and effort into the creative aspects of our message series. Three times a year, we write a sitcom that serves as the backdrop and context for a sermon series. To support the drama, we build an elaborate set. One year we turned the entire stage into a restaurant called This Place. The title of the series was I Love This Place, and the topics we covered were the seven core values of North Point Community Church:

1. Strategic Service

2. Relevant Environments

3. Intentional Apprenticing

4. Authentic Community

5. Intimacy with God

6. Relational Evangelism

7. Biblical Authority

Through this series we were able to showcase the mission and strategy of the church using a very creative and compelling backdrop.

On another occasion we built a television studio and wrote a sitcom around the characters who worked for a cable channel. The name of the series and mock television show was Surviving the Bear Market. I focused on the personal bear markets that many of us face as a result of bad life investment decisions.

Like Ed, I am a fanatic when it comes to creative communication. But I still don't have the nerve to ride a camel into church.

22

teaching less for more

Andy Stanley

*We gear our teaching for comprehension
and meeting the listeners' needs.*

Several principles guide us as we develop and manage our ministries at North Point. One principle is that the amount of information we teach should be directly related to the listeners' comprehension. Too much information can result in less learning, while less information can result in more learning and better application. People learn one thing at a time—and they remember what is repeated. The "teach less for more" principle has helped us strategically design environments where learning is focused and relevant.

Deciding What to Say

Some churches use denominational materials to drive their curriculum plan; others review all that is available before deciding what they want to teach. So many resources are available for churches to use that it would be easy to teach random topics for years and never repeat any of them. Rather than letting the curriculum drive what we teach, however, we believe it is our responsibility to decide what is important for our people to learn. Each department at North Point has determined the core of information that is important for their "season of life" group. By identifying the needs of each specific age group and then prioritizing teaching to address those needs, we have established a "bottom line" for every department that helps guide the leaders in selecting and planning curriculum.

When a department plans a production, a class, or a service, the creative process revolves around what we call a "written brief," or the main point we are trying to communicate. Having the main point determined and written down in advance ensures that our music, drama, and other creative components complement the principle we're trying to get across. It is so easy to waste enormous amounts of creative time and frustrate talented thinkers when there is no bottom line to keep ideas on track. Sometimes we plan retreats or special meetings to clarify the "written briefs" that will drive a curriculum or preaching series. But we never have a meeting to plan how we are going to say something until we have first decided what we are going to say!

Deciding What Not to Say

You can't decide what information is most important without making difficult decisions about what is not important. The "teach less for more" principle provides a strategic filter that helps us decide what not to teach. The basis for everything we communicate is the Bible. However, just because all Scripture is equally inspired doesn't mean that all Scripture is equally applicable. For example, it really doesn't make sense to:

- Describe the Beast of Revelation to preschoolers

- Talk about David's sin with Bathsheba to kindergarten children

- Do a study of the Old Testament feast days with middle school students

Teaching should be strategic and applicable. We only have a few years with our preschoolers, elementary-age children, and teenagers, and we need to streamline what we say to them. This does not mean that we should compromise the significant themes of salvation, grace, faith, or other aspects of the gospel. Those are presented in a relevant way at every age level.

Say One Thing at a Time

The "teach less for more" concept not only means that we prioritize the core of information we teach an age group, but also that we use our teaching time wisely. Traditional teaching and preaching tries to squeeze as much information as possible into a single message. Alliterated lists or numerated points are shared to instill as many principles as possible into the hearts and minds of those listening. The only problem is that people do not actually learn that way. Sometimes sharing multiple principles hinders application. We have discovered that when people walk away clearly understanding one single principle, they are much more likely to apply that principle.

Say It Over and Over

What is worth remembering is always worth repeating. For example, during the preschool years, babies and toddlers get their first impression of what their heavenly Father is like. For this reason, we have three foundational truths we want kids to understand by the time they are four years old, and we repeat them regularly. While children are in elementary school, our goal is to introduce them to a personal relationship with Jesus Christ and help them grow in wisdom and friendships. We have identified a specific set of character and faith issues that are important for them to understand by the fifth grade, and we emphasize these over and over again.

Our student staff designs all of its weekly programming and special events around seven "checkpoints" for teenagers. In every environment—including summer camps and weekend retreats—and in numerous creative ways, these seven principles are discussed repeatedly. Our goal is simple: We have decided that these are the most important things teenagers should know by the time they graduate, and we want them to have a comprehensive understanding of these issues by the time they leave our student ministry. Our leaders and staff have permission to teach these principles over and over again for the sake of ensuring application.

We also use this practice with our adult congregation. At the beginning of each year, we take the opportunity in our worship services to once again cast the vision of the church for all the members and attenders. We repeat who we are, why we are here, and where we are going—and invite them to join us.

Recycling Truth

In our worship services, as well as in our age-graded programs, establishing a cycle for repeating important principles has several advantages:

- It cooperates with the way people actually learn.

- It enhances creativity by providing focus for ideas.

- It enables production teams to be more effective in planning.

- It gives volunteers and leaders a clearer vision of our teaching priorities.

- It helps parents understand our goals for their children and teenagers.

- It ensures that newcomers and rotating attenders do not miss important principles.

At North Point, we teach less for more—and if the lives around us are any indication, people are learning.

ED'S TAKE

I agree with everything Andy says here and can't add much. I constantly challenge our staff—whether they're planning Bible study lessons, small-group studies, or a message series—to answer the most important question in any teaching environment: "So what?"

When I teach or preach, I always try to apply the Bible to daily life by asking, "So what?" For example, if I preach about faith, I had better answer the questions, "What do I need to know, and what action do I need to take?" I challenge our teachers to do the same thing. Seventy-five percent of Jesus' words had to do with application and life change. We need to follow his teaching model. If people leave your worship service without an answer to "so what?" you've wasted their time and yours.

Another challenge of teaching and preaching is hitting as many different groups of people as possible with your message. When I am studying, I try to visualize the chairs in our worship center and the types of people who sit in them. How does my message apply to single adults, married couples, empty nesters, teenagers, men, women, and so on? Obviously, you can't hit every demographic group represented in your church; but the more you hit, the better. If I am teaching a message aimed at singles and their dating relationships, I will make an effort to talk to married adults who have to teach their children about dating. If I am teaching a series on marriage, I tell singles up front that there is a 90 percent chance they will marry at least once in their lifetime—so they'd better listen and take notes.

23

integrating vision

Ed Young

We constantly incorporate the vision of our church into our messages.

We have purposely kept the vision of Fellowship Church easy to understand and remember. We exist to reach up (corporate worship of God), to reach out (evangelism and reaching the community), and to reach in (discipleship of our members). I constantly reaffirm this vision during my messages to keep it in the forefront of our members' minds.

I find that church leaders are either shy to talk about their church's vision (as though they are ashamed of it), or they assume each member already knows and understands his or her purpose. But studies show that even the most ardent followers will lose focus and forget their vision and purpose after six months. In an evangelistically driven church like Fellowship, this is especially dangerous. We want to be reaching outward to the community, but people who have forgotten their overall purpose inevitably turn in to themselves and become self-centered. Left to itself, the church will always turn inward.

Creative Casting

Vision casting does not have to be offensive, in your face, or boring. I hardly ever say directly, "And now, this is the vision of Fellowship Church." The subject comes up casually. A vision is simply the philosophy of why we do what we do; if we always have a clear idea of what that philosophy is, it shouldn't be that difficult to bring up.

I often use a subtle but invaluable method of vision casting. During the announcements I might say, "We're having a tennis clinic on Saturday. It's going to be a lot of fun and a great way to reach people, so bring your friends." That simple statement affirms the reaching-out part of our vision and encourages members to evangelize.

Or I might say in a message on loneliness, "Our HomeTeams here at Fellowship Church are our small-group ministry. We want to minister to everyone personally. If you haven't checked out a HomeTeam, I urge you to try it. It's a fantastic way to meet people and grow together in Christ. I hear all the time about someone going through a hard time, and before I can even call the person, HomeTeam members have already been to the house, brought food over, and prayed with the person. Don't miss it." This subtly reinforces our desire to be involved in discipleship through the HomeTeam ministry.

All the programs at our church tie in to the vision—from Bible studies to athletic events to children's ministries—and I give the "why" behind the "what" whenever possible. I can guarantee that I mention at least one aspect of the vision every weekend. Any message, any topic, can be tied in to the church's philosophy. This subtlety is essential, because if people feel that they are being nagged into further involvement, they will soon stop listening.

Focused Casting

I do try to devote several services a year solely to the vision of the church. I tell the guests that they've picked the best possible weekend to visit Fellowship because they're going to find out exactly what we're all about. Then I go through the vision, explaining and reaffirming it: This is what we are doing and why we are doing it, and this is where we're going. People want to know that our vision is still working, so I often read letters we've received or bring members up front to give personal testimonies of life change.

The arts team works to create the right kind of atmosphere during these messages. Because the goal is to get members excited about the vision, the music is upbeat and often includes songs about rallying together. We want to make people feel included in the vision—to feel that they are the ones making it happen. We want them to take ownership of the vision and know that it is theirs.

There are many different ways to do this. In one of my most recent vision messages, we used a sports metaphor. The music team wore baseball shirts. During one of the songs, we showed a video of all the church's athletic teams playing various sports. People saw themselves on the side screens and felt a part of what was happening. Vision is like tithing: God doesn't need your money. He needs you to be a part of what he is doing.

Leadership Benefits

Vision casting is not something I do only for the congregation. I gain a lot myself from preparing for a vision message. It refocuses me on the basics of what our church is all about and keeps me from going off on tangents.

The other leaders in our church experience the same thing when they speak on the vision for their own departments. But they also benefit from being reminded of the broader church vision. Leaders can lose sight of the overall picture when they focus only on their own ministry, like the youth department or the women's ministry. A vision message puts everyone back on track so that we're working toward the same goal. It also encourages us if we're doing well and motivates us if we need to do better.

One of the keys of effective communication is repeating yourself in a different, creative way each time. So I repeat the vision of the church in a variety of creative ways each week. I don't ever want to close out the message with a standard phrase or cliché, because people will get tired of hearing it and tune it out. Instead, I try to creatively keep the vision at the forefront of the congregation's mind so they stay motivated and excited about what we're doing. I understand that if I want people to know what Fellowship Church is all about, I have to tell them at every chance I get.

ANDY'S TAKE

I use the first three Sundays of the year for vision casting. During those weeks I focus on the Great Commission, small groups, and our invest-and-invite strategy. Then every June I do a message entitled Strategic Service. The goal of this message is to cast our vision within the context of our need for volunteers. After that service people are given an opportunity to sign up for various ministries in the church.

24

personal evaluation

Ed Young

*I watch the video of my message every weekend
and evaluate my effectiveness.*

We have three weekend worship services at Fellowship Church, one on Saturday night at 6:00 P.M. and two on Sunday morning at 9:30 and 11:15. We videotape the service and display it on side screens so that people in the balcony don't miss my goofy facial expressions (and other important things happening on the platform). I always make sure I get a copy of the tape on Saturday night, and the arts team and I watch it before we leave the church. We often make changes to the order or content of the service for the next morning. Many times I will also watch the 9:30 or 11:15 tape before I go home Sunday afternoon.

Just like the NFL

I do this to critique myself. There are too many areas where I could improve as a speaker to not challenge myself to become a better communicator. My perception of my gestures and actions is oftentimes very different from what they actually look like onstage, and I have to see them on video to get the right perspective.

Professional sports teams do this all the time. Football players spend hours with the coaches going over and over the game tape to see what they did and how they could improve it. That's my purpose too. By watching the tapes, I've recognized particular quirks—the same gestures or the same verbiage used over and over—and have intentionally stopped making those motions and using those words. I remember watching one video and hearing myself repeat, "The Bible comes along and says..." over and over. I don't want to sound like a broken record, so I stopped using that phrase. At one point I noticed that my voice was too high and too loud for long stretches of time, so I consciously made the effort to keep the volume down and vary my tone.

I've heard people say that they don't like hearing the sound of their voice on tape. Chances are that if you don't like it, no one else does either. A seminary professor once said that if you feel you have the gift of preaching, you'd better be sure your congregation has the gift of hearing you preach. And one way to ensure that is through hard work and personal evaluation. It's easy for me to get self-conscious about watching myself, but it's worth the effort if it means I can communicate God's truth more effectively.

A Team Effort

When our church was younger, the whole staff would watch the video of the entire service during a staff meeting and positively critique it. In fact, that was originally the entire purpose of our staff meetings. We discussed the message, music, drama, hospitality, and anything else we could think of. Those meetings were exhausting, but they were also essential in keeping everyone on the same page in the early days. Now that we have ten years of experience under our belts, such an exhaustive critique every week isn't as necessary.

Other Options

If your church doesn't have the capabilities for videotaping each message, then I recommend at least audiotaping them. Many churches already do this in order to make messages available after the service. Take those tapes and listen to them in your office after the service or in the car on the way home. Critique every aspect of your message: the theology, the organization, the illustrations, the clarity of thought, your enunciation. Whatever you can think of to critique, take the time to do it. Over time you will definitely see the fruit of your labor.

I always bounce ideas off other people. I might ask staff members if they've noticed me depending upon a certain expression or phrase and if that repetition is starting to become annoying. Trust me, they're always glad for the opportunity to let me know that I'm being annoying! My best sounding board is my wife, Lisa, without whom I would be lost. She is always honest with me about what I could do to improve my speaking style.

Self-criticism, in the positive sense, is one of the most difficult and yet most needed disciplines in the Christian leader's life and ministry. But I'm convinced that with eternal souls at stake, we can't afford to neglect this important habit.

ANDY'S TAKE

Howard Hendricks said it best: "Experience doesn't make you better, only evaluated experience makes you better." There is nothing I hate worse than watching my own videos. But there is nothing I know of that is more effective in helping me hone my communication skills.

At North Point, we spend a portion of each worship-service planning meeting evaluating everything that took place the previous Sunday. Every part of the service is open for discussion, including my sermon. Like Ed, I'm convinced there is no excellence without evaluation.

the history of north point community church

Alpharetta, Georgia

In November of 1995, Andy Stanley stood in front of a gathering of believers at a North Atlanta convention center and cast a unique vision. "Atlanta does not need another church," he said. "What Atlanta does need is a safe environment where the unchurched can come and hear the life-changing truth that Jesus Christ cares for them and died for their sin." So began North Point Community Church.

Andy Stanley addresses a gathering of believers to cast the vision for North Point Community Church.

For the first three and a half years of its existence, North Point met every other Sunday night in rented facilities. When the Olympics came to town in 1996, the church was unable to meet for nine weeks. "Those were our pioneering days," says Julie Arnold, Director of Service Programming. "Everybody had to pitch in and do whatever needed to be done. It was difficult to attend North Point back then, especially for families with kids. Only those who were truly committed to our mission and strategy stayed with us through those defining years."

When Andy talks about those early years, he focuses on the unique opportunity the unusual schedule afforded them. "We made a strategic decision not to focus on growth, but instead to focus on leadership development," he explains. "As a result, when we moved to our own facility and began regular Sunday morning services, we had a core of leaders who knew exactly what we were trying to do and exactly where they fit in."

Outposts in the Community

In addition to the Sunday evening services, NPCC started three ministries early on that were designed to capture the attention of their three target audiences.

KidStuf

Targeting families with elementary-aged children, KidStuf was established in a local elementary school cafeteria under the leadership of Reggie Joiner. KidStuf is a one-hour program in which children participate with their parents in a highly interactive, values-driven learning environment. As Reggie is fond of saying, "KidStuf is where kids bring their parents to church." This was North Point's first presence in the community they would later call home.

KidStuf was begun in a local elementary school cafeteria.

Today KidStuf takes place in a five-hundred-seat theatre.

InsideOut

While families gathered for KidStuf, the student ministry team was setting up five miles away in a rented recreation center for

InsideOut, an environment designed for high school students. Under the leadership of Kevin Ragsdale, the InsideOut volunteers made the church's presence known among teenagers in the area.

*InsideOut, an environment for high school students,
began in a rented recreation center.*

*Now InsideOut happens each Sunday in a theatre complete with booths,
lounge chairs, ping-pong tables, and billiards.*

7:22

After participating in a conference together, Bill Willits, Director of Group Life, and Louie Giglio of Passion Conferences, felt led to create a weekly worship and teaching environment for single adults. As a result, 7:22 was born. Under the leadership of North Point's Singles Ministry, 7:22 quickly became a gathering point for hundreds and later thousands of singles and college students from all over the state. Bill's exceptional organizational skills, combined with Louie's passion to communicate, enabled North Point to make its mark in the young-adult population of North Atlanta.

Opening Day

In December of 1996, North Point completed the purchase of an eighty-three-acre site in the middle of Alpharetta, a small town fifteen miles north of Atlanta. Six months later, construction began on what was to be the first of three building phases. The first phase of construction included a twenty-seven-hundred-seat auditorium, along with a small theater, offices, and education space for preschoolers and children.

On August 27, 1997, the staff, elders, and key leaders gathered for a groundbreaking ceremony on North Point's property in Alpharetta.

The congregation of North Point Community Church moved into their new home on September 24, 1998. That first Sunday more than two thousand adults attended two morning worship services. By Christmas, attendance had grown to three thousand. By the end of the first year, North Point was averaging more than four thousand in worship. The leadership immediately began making plans for a second phase of construction.

On April 12, 1998, Easter services were held in a tent in the middle of the construction site. This was the attenders' first opportunity to see the future home of North Point Community Church.

"It was difficult to determine what to build," says Rick Holliday, Director of Administration. "We were growing so fast that we didn't feel we had time for a three-year building campaign. Also, we had no idea how large an auditorium we would need in three years." Faced with this dilemma, the church leadership decided to experiment with multiple worship environments as a faster and less costly way to meet the immediate needs.

By spring of 2001, North Point completed its second phase of construction. In addition to more education space, more offices, and an environment designed specifically for high school students, this phase included a second auditorium that was built directly behind the original one. With the additional seating, North Point is able to accommodate five thousand worshipers at one time.

North Point Community Church's main entrance

Beyond the Numbers

Currently, North Point Community Church has more than ten thousand adults (of which three thousand are members) participating in two morning worship services. Additionally, more than three thousand

thousand children and middle school students meet in small groups while their parents attend worship. But of course, the numbers don't tell the whole story. Changed lives are what drive the leadership at North Point.

A recent worship service in North Point Community Church's main auditorium

Lane Jones, Director of Membership Development, puts it this way: "Our real mission is to lead people into a growing relationship with Jesus Christ. That's not just a slogan on our wall. We have measured our success by that standard from the beginning. If we ever stop hearing stories of life change, I guarantee we will stop what we are doing and regroup, no matter how many people are attending."

What's next at North Point? Currently the church is establishing a second campus twenty miles south of the current location. If that is successful, they are planning a third campus twenty miles north as well. These campuses will be fully programmed environments; the only exception is that the preaching element will be fed in by a yet undetermined technology.

When asked to comment on the amazing growth at North Point Community Church, Reggie Joiner, Director of Season of Life Ministries, says, "We can't explain it. We don't try to explain it. We just pray that God will keep us from getting in the way of what he's up to."

the history of fellowship church

Dallas, Texas

In 1990 a core group of Christ-followers came together and asked one simple question: How can we reach people today with the life-changing message of Jesus Christ? Through that heart for people and a desire to communicate God's unchanging truth in creative and innovative ways, the ministry of Fellowship Church was launched. Since that time Fellowship has become a caring Christian community in the Dallas/Fort Worth area, with more than fifteen thousand in weekend attendance.

Today Fellowship Church offers a wide range of creative activities and ministries for all ages and interests. From hard-hitting weekend messages to insightful Power Source Bible studies, from HomeTeams for married and single adults to a full array of seasonal sports activities, from adult Connection classes to Adventure World for kids, and from cutting-edge student ministries to exciting college and singles ministries, everything we do at Fellowship is designed to bring people into a closer relationship with God and others.

It's a God Thing

Perhaps the best way to explain the meteoric growth of Fellowship Church is to say, "It's a God thing." Fellowship started as an extension of an existing church in Irving, Texas, when a committed group of families determined to plant a new church in the northern part of the city. The group began meeting in an office complex with about 150 people. Ed Young became the pastor in February of 1990 and immediately began to focus the mission of the young church on reaching out to the unchurched community.

Services were held in an office complex in north Irving when the church officially began in 1990.

In 1994 the church began looking for a site to build a permanent facility. Initially, the leadership thought that thirty to thirty-five acres of property would be more than adequate to meet their current needs and provide for future growth. However, God had different plans. A senior pastor from a large Midwestern church (one that had experienced a growth pattern similar to Fellowship's) advised the leadership to think bigger. Based on Fellowship's explosive growth over the previous four years, he told Ed Young, the church needed to be thinking of acreage in triple digits.

In October of 1990, the church had to move from its office location to the 750-seat Irving Arts Center across the street. While in the Arts Center, the church grew from a few hundred attendees to more than three thousand. By 1996, four identical services were being offered each weekend to provide room for the growing numbers.

But one-hundred-plus acres of land in the expensive metroplex of Dallas/Fort Worth seemed way out of the financial realm of possibility for the four-year-old church. The leaders at Fellowship knew that a land deal of such proportions could only happen if God made it happen.

After an intensive search of the local real estate market, a potential site was located in Grapevine, about three miles north of the Dallas/Fort Worth airport. The church placed a bid, but since the land was in a prime commercial spot, the leadership didn't really expect to be the highest bidder. As it turned out, it wasn't—but God strategically allowed the bid to win anyway. The church was able to secure 160 acres of prime property for $2.5 million.

The next challenge was to come up with the money. Miraculously, through the generosity of his people, God provided $800,000 in cash for the land, and financing was secured for the rest. The church began a Build the Vision campaign to pay for the property and raise money for a future building—a building that would not be built and occupied for another four years.

Part of God's provision came shortly after Fellowship signed the deal on the site. Just across the highway from the Grapevine property, construction was about to begin on the Grapevine Mills Mall, soon to be the largest outlet mall in Texas and one of the largest malls in the country. This was, of course, a catalyst for other businesses—restaurants, hotels, and other retail stores—and property values soared. Two years later, in 1996, without even putting a "For Sale" sign on the land, Fellowship sold twenty-three acres for exactly what they owed at that time—$1.75 million.

On the Move

As the plans for building permanent facilities went forward, Fellowship continued to grow beyond the capacity of the Irving Arts Center. The church had to make an interim move. So in October of 1996, Fellowship began meeting in MacArthur High School, a facility that held twelve hundred people. During the eighteen months there, church attendance grew to five thousand people each weekend.

In October 1996, the church moved to MacArthur High School across from the Arts Center.

Because the school space was leased only for the weekends, the church had to move in and set up everything that was needed for the services and children's programs (props, sets, sound equipment, instruments, risers, temporary walls, cribs, toys, mats chairs, tables, and more) and then tear down and move everything out on Sunday afternoon. This required a tremendous effort by dozens of volunteers. A Saturday evening service was also added in an existing movie theater across the street from the high school.

In 1996 a Saturday service was added in an existing movie theater across the street from the high school.

In the fall of 1996, construction began on a 125,000-square-foot building on the Grapevine property, along with a 25,000-square-foot children's building. Fellowship Church moved into its new facilities on April 5, 1998, with more than seven thousand people attending the opening weekend services.

Fellowship Church moved into its current location on April 5, 1998.

More than 7,000 people attended on the opening weekend.

In 1999 the church bought a forty-thousand-square-foot existing building located next to the property and renovated it into a youth facility and office space. This state-of-the-art facility, called the Apex, includes basketball cages, a game room, a rock-climbing wall, a cafe, and a one-thousand-seat auditorium for junior and senior high students.

The Apex houses a state-of-the-art junior and senior high student facility and additional office space.

Fellowship of the Future

Fellowship Church is currently involved in a two-year Get in the Game expansion program to provide more educational space for children and adults, a wedding chapel, an expanded atrium for fellowship, and a new road to provide better access to the campus from the south. Future construction plans also include a lake, an amphitheater, and a sports complex. Since the church is up again to four identical weekend services, two on Saturday and two on Sunday, long-range plans include a new and larger auditorium adjoining the expanded atrium. These additions to the campus will not only meet critical current needs but also prepare Fellowship for future ministry potential.

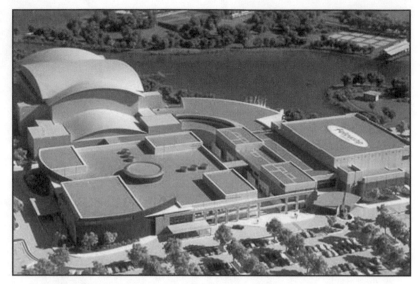

Hundreds of families are committing over the next two years to help Fellowship build a Creative Communications Center, expand the atrium, and build a new access road to the south of the campus.

As great as Fellowship's past has been, its leadership believes the prospects for the future are even more exciting. According to senior pastor Ed Young, "Fellowship Church is poised on the brink of a new millennium, ready to take the life-changing message of Jesus Christ to thousands of people who desperately need to hear it." Through radio, television, and the launch of the fellowshipchurch.com Web site, the church hopes to impact people all over the Dallas/Fort Worth area and potentially around the world for Christ. Says Young, "We're looking for men, women, and children who want to become a part of this incredible, far-reaching God thing that's happening at Fellowship Church."